Beauty from

Journeys of Recovery from the Rwandan
Genocide

Dr Callum Henderson

Authentic

24 23 22 21 20 19 18   9 8 7 6 5 4 3

First published 2007 by Authentic Media.
Reprinted 2014, 2018 by Authentic Media Limited
PO Box 6326, Bletchley, Milton Keynes, MK1 9GG.
www.authenticmedia.co.uk

British Library Cataloguing in Publication Data

A catalogue record for this book is available from the
British Library

ISBN 978-1-85078-722-8
978-1-78078-278-2 (e-book)

Cover Design by David McNeill
Printed and bound by CPI Group (UK) Ltd., Croydon, CR0 4YY

Contents

Acknowledgements

I wish to thank all those who have allowed their stories to form part of this book, and to honour your bravery and integrity. This book is for you, that your story would glorify God.

To Jean and Viviane Gakwandi and Paul and Odette Ndahigwa and their families and friends – you have been the truest friends I could ask for.

Many others, including Louis and Winnie Muvunyi, Lesley Bilinda, Nicolas and Elsie Hitimana, the late Charles Karinda, Straton Gataha and Emmanuel Kayijuka have been part of my introduction and journey to the land of a thousand hills.

Thank you, Denise, for so much help, and my thanks to the staff and volunteers at Solace, too many to mention but not too many to love, who have showered me with love and support.

Thank you to the pastors and members of *L'Église Vivante* who have welcomed and blessed me whenever I have been among them.

My thanks to my children Gregor, Ailidh and Angus for their interest and encouragement at every stage of writing. My wife Izzy is the perfect partner to support my love of Rwanda. She was joined by Siubhan, Jonathan and Val in providing helpful suggestions and advice.

I would like to thank Authentic Media and Charlotte Hubback for their support and help.

Foreword

There are moments in history so horrific that on the scale of suffering and trauma, the seismic nature of pain involved in them is incalculable. The Holocaust serves as one example of this and the genocide in Rwanda is another.

When I first read the powerful and well-researched manuscript by my friend and colleague Dr Callum Henderson, I found myself recoiling from the pages. The account seemed too vivid a portrayal of the sadistic violence meted out to a powerless community. There are few pastel shades in the following pages: the prose portrays the killing fields of a persecuted people in stark primary colours.

The problem is that the West has become anaesthetised to acute anguish on a national scale. News images that once appalled have become the daily diet of a pampered people desensitised by the comparative comfort and protection that we enjoy. This book brings the harrowing 'out there' a little closer to home.

Whenever I visit areas of the world scarred by poverty or persecution, and see the deep furrows that have been etched with an iron pen onto the psyche of a people who deserve better, I resolve never to grumble again – yet inevitably I do. Images we believe to be indelible too easily fade from our consciousness as the routine of the ordinary recaptures our attention.

Not a few may ask how God could have allowed the Rwandan tragedy to occur without his intervention.

I remember once reading that God rarely answers the question why, for the person who asks why usually doesn't want an explanation – they want an argument. The question should not be: 'Why do bad things happen to good people?' The question should really be: 'What happens to good people when bad things happen to them?'

On the wall of a German home next to a star of David were found the words: 'I believe in the sun even when it is not shining.'

Callum Henderson encourages us beyond the darkness to the other side of 'shadow' and reveals that there has never been a place so dark that God cannot penetrate with sunlight. These are moving accounts of forgiveness and reconciliation – most of them demonstrating a gradual process rather than an instant victory. Incubation takes place as God brings faith to the right temperature in order that new life can be born out of the travail of wounded lives.

John Glass

Glossary

CDR
Coalition for the Defence of the Republic. Hutu extremist splinter party of the ruling MRND.
Promoted violent anti-Tutsi activity.

Cell (French *cellule*)
Smallest of the four Rwandan administrative units, usually containing less than a thousand people.

District (French **commune**)
Second level of Rwandan administrative structure.

Gakwandi, Jean
Director of Solace Ministries, a Christian organisation set up to help widows and orphans.
His story is told in chapter 21.

Gendarmerie
A paramilitary police force of six thousand, trained by Belgian and French advisors, and deeply involved in the genocide. Often used when the killing was met by resistance.

Genocidaire
A French word used to describe someone who participated in the genocide, and generally used in Rwanda for
this purpose in all languages.

Interahamwe
The armed youth militia wing of the ruling Mouvement
Révolutionaire National pour le Développement party
(MRND).

MRND
Mouvement Révolutionaire National pour le
Développement – National Revolutionary Movement
for Development. The ruling party in Rwanda from 1975
to 1994, without opposition parties until shortly before
the genocide.

Operation Turquoise
A military operation by the French which established
part of the south-west of Rwanda under their control
towards the end of the genocide.

Pit latrine
Most rural houses and many urban ones do not have
flushing toilets. A pit anything up to twenty feet deep
is dug, with a slab for squatting put across the top.
During the genocide, the slab was removed and bodies, sometimes still alive, were thrown down the pit.
When filled with bodies, the pits were topped with
mud. Many bodies are still being retrieved from
them.

President Habyarimana
Leader of MRND and President of Rwanda from 1973 to
1994. On 6 April 1994 he was killed when his private jet,

a gift from President Jacques Chirac, was shot down. An hour later the genocide began.

Province (French **préfecture**)
Rwanda was divided into twelve provinces which have now been reduced to four plus Kigali city.

RPF
Rwandan Patriotic Front. After several years of trying by peaceful means to re-enter Rwanda, refugees from the early years of ethnic tension and killing formed an army to force entry. In October 1990 they launched an offensive, gaining some ground in the north before they were repulsed by government and French soldiers. They continued to hold some ground in the north-east until the genocide began, and under the terms of a 'peace treaty' they also had a contingent based in Kigali.

RTLM
Radio Télévision Libre de Mille Collines – Independent Radio Television of a Thousand Hills. Radio station that spewed out extremist anti-Tutsi propaganda and incited the genocide. Rwanda is known as 'The Land of a Thousand Hills', hence the name of the station.

Sector (French *secteur*)
The third level of Rwandan administration, in populous areas of several square kilometres.

SOS
An orphanage. The full name is Villages d'Enfants SOS du Rwanda.

Twa

The Ba'Twa or Twa people are a pygmy group forming less than 1 per cent of the population of Rwanda. Originally hunter-gatherers, they have gradually been displaced from their indigenous areas and many are among the poorest in Rwanda.

Introduction

There is a certain irony in how the world has dealt with the Rwandan genocide. Seldom can there have been so little action taken in the face of such great need as during the events of 1994. Yet in the years following the genocide, and particularly since the publicity of the tenth anniversary of 1994 in 2004, there has been a growing interest and involvement with the restoration of this small, densely-populated African country. Rwanda has moved from its customary role as an unheard-of African nation to being the focus of considerable attention, including a significant number of major Christian initiatives such as Rick Warren's *Purpose-Driven Nation* and Hillsong's *100 Days of Hope*.

Much of this interest and involvement, which Rwandans receive with their customary grace and warm welcome, is due to the way that Rwanda has made herself many friends among the nations, because of the open and honest way in which she has faced and owned up to the tragedy. Whether there is a real desire on the part of other governments and peoples to know the facts of the genocide and to learn from them is unclear. The twentieth century was the worst in the history of mankind for pointless slaughters of humanity, with millions being killed outside the realms of what could be termed war.[1] The opportunities to learn how not to repeat such tragedies have regularly been passed by. No amount of aid after the event can bring back those who died, and the reluctance of western countries to take decisive action in Darfur, Sudan would indicate that mopping up the mess is still preferred by many to preventative intervention.

But Rwanda is teaching people everywhere how to turn from such horror and to transform a nation through comfort, peace and reconciliation. It is greatly to Rwanda's credit that she should so openly invite the rest of the world to share in her recovery. A people with less humility could say with justification: 'You failed us in our hour of need, why should you expect to be included in our hour of blessing?'

My own involvement in Rwanda is largely with Christians. Although over ninety per cent of Rwandans claim Christianity as their 'religion', there are many fewer who accept the Lordship of Christ and want to live as his disciples. Rwandans are special people, but those belonging to the true church of Christ in that country are exceptional. Kind, generous, thoughtful, humble, gracious, patient, zealous for God; these are just a few of the words that come to mind. Above all, they are exceptionally lavish in their welcome. Many times I, and others I have introduced to Rwanda, have been told 'Even if you have brought with you nothing to help us, your presence is enough because it tells us you are thinking of us and you love us.' Rwandans are a people who are making the most of the help they are receiving, working hard to reconstruct their nation and heal the wounded souls of the genocide.

However, they do want their story to be told and giving the Rwandan people, especially the widows and orphans, the opportunity to speak of their experiences and recovery through these pages is part of the healing process. It is their desire to share their testimony of horror and hope, for they know that no one can truly understand and relate to them without first knowing the deep, dark canyon through which they have travelled to get to where they are now.

One of the survivors whose story is told in this book, Uwineza, sums up those feelings: 'I'm glad that now I can share my feelings and especially my story. When people listen to me, they also encourage me, and now I realise I have a new beginning in my life. I feel relieved, and my wish is that others in the same situation would be comforted as I have been. I thank God.' They want the world to know how much they have suffered, and to respond to that knowledge by ministering God's comfort to those who survived. They want the world to know how powerful God is to heal the wounds and restore the soul. And they want the world to know that despite all it has heard about genocide and cruelty and terrible suffering, there is much of Jesus to be found in the people of Rwanda.

While I was taking a group of Christians around the country recently, one of them kept having visions of Jesus standing and sitting among the people. Wherever she went she saw Jesus there and the impression that God made on her heart was this: it is not we who are taking Jesus to Rwanda; it is we who are discovering him among the people.

The stories in this book are designed to help you discover Jesus among the Rwandan people: healing, restoring and empowering. And as you discover Jesus among the Rwandans, you will discover the God of hope who can take a shattered nation, wash it, heal it, and hold it up to the world as a demonstration of his wonderful grace.

1

Horror and Hope

In 1994 Mukagatare Esperance's*² world came crashing down. She is one individual among the multitudes in Rwanda who were never to be the same again by the end of those three, terror-filled months that wiped out a million Rwandans and left countless others traumatised, bereaved, orphaned, widowed, raped, mutilated, scarred or jailed. So many women endured the double trauma of watching their family and relatives killed and themselves being viciously raped. For Esperance the method of abuse was horrifyingly brutal: after being attacked, thrown into a river to drown and dragged out alive, she was tied to a tree and repeatedly raped. Many died like this, but she survived.

It is 2004, and ten years on, Esperance is still living in the shadow of her past, the emotions numbed but the trauma still there. Today she is visiting a friend. *'Mwaramutse'* (good morning) she greets her friend, who calls back *'Mwaramutse neza'* (it is a good morning). As Esperance walks into the house, her eyes adjusting to the dark interior of the poorly lit room after the glare of the hot bright African sun, she does not suspect anyone else is there. Suddenly she catches sight of a man's face,

unforgettably familiar – the face of the man that tied her
to the tree and raped her. Her legs buckle and everything goes black. It takes less than an instant for all the
fear, the brutality, the shocking defencelessness, the terror of death to come rushing back to her heart and in a
moment she collapses into a coma lasting for three days.
When she awakes, it will take almost two years before
she can speak again.

Such is the legacy of trauma that fills hundreds of thousands of hearts in Rwanda. There are hundreds of
thousands of such people who walk the streets of
Rwanda and fill its jails, and hundreds of thousands
of hearts that need healing. Many have written their lives
off, pessimistically ascribing any hope to the next generation: as for them, they say, life finished in 1994.

But God has not finished with any generation and is
constantly surprising the lost and lonely with his love
and hope. 'Comfort, O comfort My people,' the prophet
Isaiah declares. 'Speak kindly to Jerusalem; and call out
to her that her warfare has ended, that her iniquity has
been removed . . . a voice is calling, clear the way for the
Lord' (Is. 40:1-3). There is little doubt that Rwanda has
paid a high price for a deep descent into hatred and violence after the heady days of a revival that touched large
parts of East Africa in the 1930s and 40s. But where sin
abounds, grace abounds all the more, and the grace of
God that is touching Rwanda is a grace that comforts,
heals and restores.

From the top of government to the multitudes of
brave individuals tackling poverty and the legacy of
genocide, God is present in power and grace. The
President, Paul Kagame, regularly joins the many
Christian MPs to pray and ask God to heal the nation.
But it is the ordinary men and women of Rwanda, who
fill its streets with bright coloured garments and its air

with the sound of singing, that God is using to change the nation.

There is a well-known verse in Psalm 30 that says: 'Weeping may last for the night'. The Hebrew words say: 'Weeping comes in at evening to lodge'. In the years following the genocide it sometimes seemed that the dark night of weeping had lodged for a lifetime, but God's compassion is bringing a dawn to light that casts its warming glow on a beautiful country and a beautiful people.

In an age when tragedies, disasters and wars melt off our TV screens under the hot stage light of the next headline, we are apt to forget that deep wounds do not heal quickly. The trauma of Rwanda spanned three generations. The elderly, the working-age population and the children and youth were all affected. No one was safe because of age – babies and infants were killed to make sure they did not grow up to be Tutsi soldiers in the next generation. Those who survived saw and heard enough to affect them for a lifetime.

Like Esperance, Uwimbabazi Nadia was deeply traumatised by what she heard and saw. She was nine years old and had already been sent to her godmother for safety before the genocide began. Her father was suspected, wrongly, of sympathies with the Rwandan Patriotic Front who were invading the north of the country. Her godmother's husband was also accused and then arrested and killed in prison for the same reason, and once the genocide began her father, mother and three brothers and sisters were all killed. She herself was found and taken to a pit that served as a mass grave. The killers had collected about twenty people, and started to beat them one by one with clubs and throw the bodies into the trench. As they attacked a young girl next to Nadia with a machete, some others started to kick her.

As she fell into a gutter near the trench, she passed out with the shock and lay unconscious for two days. 'God saved me from death!' she concludes.

Over the next year Nadia regularly planned suicide, without success. On one such occasion, as she was walking to the place where she had planned to take her life, a young Christian girl felt compelled by God to approach her and pray with her. 'I went with her,' Nadia says, 'and she said God had revealed to her that I was planning to do something wrong and that she had to pray for me. She prayed, and after that we talked; I told her what I was about to do and I fainted for about an hour.'

The trauma experienced by survivors was constantly erupting and hitting them in all kinds of situations. In the post-genocide years, children were taught in schools how to close their desks quietly, as some children would pass out from fear and fall on the floor if a desk lid closed unexpectedly.

During those dark months of the genocide, Lt General Romeo Dallaire, the Force Commander for the United Nations Assistance Mission for Rwanda (UNAMIR) witnessed and experienced what he has called 'the living experience of hell.'[3] When he talks of Rwanda, his passionate anger at the inertia and self-interest of the world community merges with a vivid picture of the unfolding tragedy.

But what is clear is his agreement with the many in Rwanda who see behind the human degradation and the undoubted responsibility of those who took part to the work of demonic forces. 'Literally, the devil took over the country,' he says. 'You are literally talking about Lucifer personifying evil.' And again: 'I felt myself literally shaking hands with the devil incarnated in those men.' The involvement of the devil does not excuse the responsibility of those who committed acts of genocide, despite the attempts of some to use it that way. But it is a warning that when the devil sows enough hatred among a people, the overflow of evil will leave none untouched.

Such evil cannot be imagined. It is impossible to think oneself into the place of those who walked through this genocide, scraping by the narrowest of margins back into the world of the living. They experienced the fear of certain death by machete, the horror of watching helplessly as friends and family were buried alive, burnt to death, sexually mutilated; parents forced to watch their children's arms and legs being cut off, the stench of hundreds of thousands of decaying bodies, the stomach-churning log jams of bodies floating downriver, the moans and gasps of wounded victims begging for death, the sickening sight of heaps of women raped to death, the helpless last gasp of babies ripped from the wombs of pregnant mothers. Such things are the work of the thief, the liar, the murderer, the devil.

All over the country the memorials stacked with thousands of dry bones and skulls still fail to touch the surface of what it was like to live through such a dark tunnel of sadistic killing, torture and fear. It is the bottom of the valley of death, and those who survived looked into the very jaws of hell. And still the trauma continues as, year after year, remains are located and exhumed for decent burial. As I write this, I am again in Rwanda as chairman of the charity Comfort Rwanda visiting our partners there. It is Christmas 2005 and seventeen thousand people have just been laid to rest at Gasabo. Three hundred and fifty bodies have just been found in pit latrines at Masoro, and seven hundred and fifty at Kabuga. The Gisozi memorial in Kigali is closed for more burials today to add to the 256,000 already there. Tomorrow I will be at Mugina where thirty thousand were killed and remains are being recovered from the bush and retrieved from stray dogs for burial in a new memorial, and the next day I will sit at Karama where twenty thousand died, and I will breathe the foul stench of freshly exhumed remains heaped on a pile in the room at my back.

Original estimates of a quarter of a million killed were revised to half a million, and then to a million as census figures and mass graves continued to provide fresh evidence of the scale of the disaster. Official Government sources now put the figure at 'more than a million.'[4] Large numbers of remains are still being uncovered as confessions of prisoners yield new information and the final figure of those killed, though never likely to be precisely known, may continue to rise.

After 1994 the people of Rwanda lay stunned and devastated, unable to believe their own country had descended into such chaos and carnage, reeling from their pain and loss. Such horror does not disappear from the lives of the millions who experienced it when it moves to the annals of history. It cries out for relief from their hearts, hearts weighed down under the burden of pain and wearied by the toil of poverty.

It is not enough for a lesson to be learned. Those who survived are walking the streets and hoeing the fields of Rwanda today, and must be ministered to and brought to the love of God in the cross of Jesus for healing. Many have cause to doubt the church – there were too many church leaders with little or nothing of the true gospel in their hearts who stood by and watched, participated in or even organised the genocide. It is the radical truth of a gospel of good news, love and reconciliation that is needed by those who suffered.

It is because of this that the glory of God must be seen. The church in Rwanda wants the world to know God is at work. 'It is not as people think,' they say. 'We are one in Christ.' The gospel is not a creed or religion; it is news of something massively good. It is especially something good for the poor, the orphan and the widow, and Rwanda has an abundance of those. It is the arrival of good in the midst of hopelessness, and it has to have the answer to the questions that arise rapid-fire from those who have survived in Rwanda and those who have looked on in bewilderment. And it has an answer that shouts back at those of us in the church of Jesus Christ who have grown accustomed to maintenance theology and club-like Christianity. It tells us that where God is allowed to be God, he has the answers. He is able to do far more than shelter a chorus-singing group from the harsh realities of a materialist, self-worshipping culture. The work God is carrying out in Rwanda is healing, delivering, restoring and providing for thousands and thousands of his people.

At the end of his riveting account *Shake Hands With the Devil*,[5] General Dallaire encourages 'young authors, journalists and scholars to study this human tragedy and to contribute to our growing understanding of the genocide. If we do not understand what happened, how will we ever ensure it does not happen again?' It is my belief that the work of God in the restoration of shattered lives in Rwanda is a vital contribution, helping us not just to understand what happened but to understand what is now happening on the ground amongst the ordinary survivors. The church has rightly been castigated for its inept and heartless response to the growing culture of racial hatred; it is only right that the work of healing and hope that God is doing through a renewed church is seen in the public arena. Authors like Meg Guillebaud[6] and Lesley Bilinda[7] have brought some of those stories to light and it is my hope that the testimonies you read in this book will also bring glory to God.

Wherever there are people there is brokenness, bondage and sickness. When Jesus came he brought good news and declared that 'the kingdom of God has come near' (Mk. 1:15). The message of this book is that when good news comes to the poor, the power of hell to maintain its grip on its victims is broken. Out of the awful empty despair, the healing balm of God fills the hearts of survivors and gives new hope and life. The journey is a long one but the brave survivors of Rwanda, who have mourned as no others have mourned, are finding comfort and even joy and laughter from the hand of God.

In that wonderful passage in Isaiah 61 concerning the anointing on Jesus to bring good news to the poor, the promise continues

> Giving them a garland of ashes,
> The oil of gladness instead of mourning,
> The mantle of praise instead of fainting.
> So they will be called oaks of righteousness,
> The planting of the Lord, that He may be glorified.

This is the heart of God, to take broken hearts and fill them with the miracle of his healing, hope and joy. And every time that happens to a widow or orphan of Rwanda, the kingdom of God is here and God is glorified.

For Esperance, there was also hope. She relived her trauma when she came face to face with the rapist, but more than a year later she became involved with a Christian association of pineapple growers in the province of Gitarama, south-west of the capital Kigali. She met one of the facilitators of the group, Nicolas Hitimana. Although she had seen a doctor about her trauma she found the heart of God revealed in genuine love in Nicolas and his wife, Elsie. During the genocide

Nicolas had been told the killers were coming for Elsie, a Tutsi, the next day and he could either hand her over or be killed with her. God intervened and Nicolas managed to get a false Hutu ID card for her. They both escaped, although Elsie lost her father, brothers and nearly all her other blood relatives. After being funded by the Charles Bilinda Memorial Trust to study in Scotland, they have chosen to return to Rwanda with their three children and work among surviving widows and orphans and among the poverty-trapped prostitutes of Kigali. Nicolas and Elsie did not offer vain gospel platitudes but took Esperance home and welcomed her with a demonstration of Christ's love for the broken. They began to pray and minister to her, breaking the power of the attackers over her life in prayer and surrounding her with genuine, compassionate love. The fear in Esperance began to recede and she was set free from being struck dumb.

There was a time when Nicolas asked God, 'Why was I born in this time of the genocide?' The answer was the same as for Esther, and for any who are called of God for times of national need: 'You were born for such a time as this' (Esth. 4:14). It was Nicolas whose transparency, brokenness and tears at a meeting of Rwandans in Detmold, Germany, paved the way for the early document of confession and repentance circulated among Rwandan Christians that is quoted in chapter 3. As God confirmed the call on their lives to minister his healing love to the survivors, the joy of being part of God's answer took hold. 'It is a time of hope and great transformation and tremendous encouragement,' Nicolas says with passion and conviction. 'We still need to go deeper into the wounds because they are not healed at individual, community or national level, and the church needs to lead. But I am so glad to be helping in some small way.'

2

Forty Years of Ferment: One Hundred Days of Slaughter

There is a temptation to narrow down the Rwandan genocide to a crude tribal outbreak of violence, one tribe the villain, one tribe the victim. 'The Hutus killed the Tutsis, didn't they?' It is true that the genocide was greatly aided by the growth of the 'Hutu Power' movement which called for the eradication of the Tutsis. But such a simplistic understanding leaves many questions. Why were there so many mixed marriages? Why were many Hutus killed as well as Tutsis? Why were some of the leaders of the Rwandan Patriotic Front who fought the Hutu militias themselves Hutus? Colonial, political and economic factors, as well as the aforementioned spiritual authority given to hatred, violence and murder, all played a part in building pressure in this beautiful country.

Rwanda, in the days when Africa was parcelled up with neat lines and handed over to colonial powers, was given to the Germans in 1884. At that time, not one German had yet set foot in Rwanda. During the First World War, Rwanda was given to the Belgians, after the defeat of Germany in Africa. The Belgians discovered a feudal system in Rwanda in which the cattle-owning Tutsis tended to be the landowners. In a strict sense, the Tutsis and Hutus were not distinct tribes, as movement could take place between tribes, depending on a person's social and economic status; the two groups shared the same homeland and intermarried freely. Paul Ndahigwa, Vice President of *L'Église Vivante* (The Living Church) in Rwanda, puts it this way: 'Unity in diversity made our nation stronger . . . But the system that seemed to have made society united was destroyed by the influence of colonial masters.'

Rwandans, like the rest of humanity, were no angels before colonisation and the formation of the country as an expanding kingdom had not been without bloodshed, nor was its feudal system which favoured Tutsis without injustice. Nevertheless, despite their differences in status, tribal relationships were largely friendly; together they were *Banyarwandans* – the people of Rwanda.

The Belgians, however, exploited the feudal system in order to impose their administrative and economic systems onto the country more easily. Many of the early Europeans were from aristocratic backgrounds and highly favoured the Tutsis with their taller, apparently finer features. They even started a myth that attributed those finer features to a descent from Christian Ethiopians, which allowed the church to be implicated in the process of establishing racial superiority among the Tutsis. It must be said, though, that there were many godly missionaries, especially of the 'Ruanda Mission' as it was then, who avoided such talk and sought to teach and practise true Christian unity without any racial bias. As is true so often, Christianity as organised religion has failed badly where Christ as Lord and Saviour has gloriously succeeded.

The Belgians enlisted the Tutsis in the governance of Rwanda, giving them special privileges and using them to oil the machinery of colonialism. They declared that 'the government should endeavour to maintain and consolidate traditional cadres composed of the Tutsi ruling class, because of its important qualities, its undeniable intellectual superiority and its ruling potential.'[8] In 1933 the Belgians introduced identity cards which required everyone to have themselves registered by their 'tribe', which was then marked on the identity card. Those identity cards were still in use in the 1990s and became a principal tool of the *genocidaires* who used them to distinguish those they would kill from those they would spare.

Even before the genocide in 1994, some Tutsis sought Hutu identity cards to assure them of a job they were in danger of losing, or to protect them from bullying, prejudice or attack; and during the killing Tutsis sought desperately to get their hands on an identity card marked 'Hutu' which would save their life.

Shortly after the introduction of identity cards in 1933, the division between Tutsi and Hutu was arbitrarily established: those with ten cattle or more were categorised as Tutsis and the rest as Hutus, which put an end to the aspirations of Hutus to acquire Tutsi status; so a social and economic distinction became tribal and divisive. The introduction of identity cards, the arbitrary division of the population into Tutsi and Hutu, the colonial rulers' favouritism towards the Tutsis at the expense of involving or educating the Hutu majority and the inevitable power vacuum that colonialism always left in its wake were major reasons for the bloodshed that began in 1959 as independence loomed.

When the demand for independence began it was promoted mainly by a political party called the *Union*

Nationale Rwandaise (UNAR) which was formed largely by people from the Tutsi-dominated ruling elite. The Belgian authorities, fearing the rise of this pro-independence movement, hastily switched sides and nurtured another party among the Hutus called *Parmehutu*, which was founded on a sectarian ethnic ideology. Under Belgian supervision, the first massacres of Tutsis at the hands of the *Parmehutu* occurred in 1959. With Belgian support, *Parmehutu* abolished the Tutsi monarchy, which had co-existed with the colonial system, amidst widespread violence. The legacy of fear and bitterness from those days, along with the continued conviction of the Hutus that if they did not fight they would again be subjected to Tutsi domination as in colonial days, stoked the fires of ethnic conflict which exploded in 1994.

It was a policy of 'divide and rule' that created divisions so deep they would eventually spiral out of control. One of the songs sung by the Rwandan Patriotic Front (which was formed by exiles in Uganda and became the new government of Rwanda after the genocide) captured this policy eloquently

> It is the white man who has caused all that, children of
> Rwanda.
> He did it in order to find a secret way to pillage us.
> When they arrived, we were living side by side in har-
> mony.
> They were unhappy that they could not find a way to
> divide us.
> They invented different origins for us, children of
> Rwanda:
> Some were supposed to have come from Chad, others
> from Ethiopia.
> We were a fine tree, its parts all in accord, children of
> Rwanda.

> Some of us were banished abroad, to never come back.
> We were separated by this division, children of Rwanda,
> But we have overcome the whiteman's trap...
> So, children of Rwanda, we are all called to unite our
>   strength to build Rwanda.[9]

Unsurprisingly, the increasing oppression of the Hutu majority produced a simmering resentment among them which began to boil over as independence approached in 1962. From 1959 the Hutus were enabled by the Belgians to begin a process of usurping the power previously given to the Tutsis. Widespread house-burning, looting and cattle slaughtering ensued, as well as frequent killings, and hundreds of thousands of Tutsis fled to neighbouring countries, especially Uganda and Tanzania. For the next thirty-five years leading up to the genocide, sporadic outbreaks of violence against the Tutsis occurred at varying levels of severity, claiming thousands of lives.

Under Milton Obote and Idi Amin, Uganda became more intolerant of the refugees and started to force them back to Rwanda, where they were refused entry, put in camps or killed. Increasingly marginalised in Uganda, even after siding with the victorious Museveni as he overthrew Obote following his second period in office, the Rwandan refugees first formed the Rwandan Alliance for National Unity, a political party set up to find a solution to the twin problems of the refugees' status in Uganda and the dictatorship in Rwanda. After repeated failures to make progress it began to organise into an armed force, the 'Rwandan Patriotic Front' (RPF), using arms obtained from the Museveni campaign. In the early 1990s the RPF pushed into northern Rwanda. An uneasy stand-off followed and peace talks between the RPF and the Rwandan government, led by the dictator President Habyarimana, took place in Arusha, Tanzania. But already the seeds of the genocide had been sown and underneath the appearance of political progress, preparations were being made for the elimination of the Tutsis.

Over time those advocating Hutu power became more organised and developed a clear ideology encapsulated in the Ten Commandments of the Bahutu (Bahutu being the full name for the Hutus)

1. Hutus must know that the Tutsi wife is serving the Tutsi group. In consequence any Hutu who does the following is a traitor:
   a acquires a Tutsi wife
   b acquires a Tutsi mistress
   c acquires a Tutsi secretary or dependant.

2. All Hutus must know that our Hutu daughters are more worthy, conscientious, beautiful, good and sincere than those of the Tutsi.

3. Hutu women, be vigilant and bid your husbands, brothers and sons to come to their senses.

4. Hutus must know that Tutsis are dishonest in business. Their only goal is ethnic superiority. In consequence, any Hutu who does the following is a traitor:
   a forms an alliance in business with a Tutsi
   b invests money in a Tutsi company
   c lends to or borrows from a Tutsi
   d grants favours in business such as import licences, bank loans etc. to Tutsis.

5. Strategic political, economic, military and security posts must be reserved for Hutus.

6. Primary, secondary and tertiary education posts must be reserved for the Hutu.

7. The armed forces should be reserved for the Hutu.

8. The Hutu must stop taking pity on the Tutsi.

9. Hutus must be united, constantly looking for friends and allies for the Hutu cause, constantly opposing Tutsi propaganda, and being strong and vigilant against the Tutsi enemy.

10. Hutu ideology must be taught and widely spread to all Hutus.[10]

In the early nineties a worrying trend occurred in the more extreme anti-Tutsi political parties. Groups of young men belonging to the ruling MRND (*Mouvement Révolutionnaire National pour le Développement* – National Revolutionary Movement for Development) party began to organise themselves into militia groups, particularly the *interahamwe*, which means 'those who gather or attack together.' At that time a census was conducted which indicated that 90.4 per cent of the population were Hutu, 8.2 per cent Tutsi and 0.4 per cent Twa, although the number of Tutsis was probably under-reported because many Tutsis registered as Hutus to avoid discrimination. Other sources estimate figures closer to 85 per cent and 14 per cent for Hutu and Tutsi respectively, with intermarriage making concise figures difficult and partly irrelevant.

The country began to import arms in quantity, both weapons and explosives, which flooded in from around the world. The arms included a $12 million deal with a French company with the loan reportedly guaranteed by the French government. Despite official denials, France's role in the genocide bears sad reading. Its desire to maintain influence over French-speaking countries, particularly Rwanda through Habyarimana's regime, has led to massive ethical compromises. Although some individual French citizens and soldiers acted with integrity, the International Federation for Human Rights, the European Court of Human Rights and the Rwandan envoy to the International Criminal Tribunal for Rwanda have all accused France of human rights failures in connection with the genocide, including a considerable reluctance to prosecute genocide suspects taking refuge in France.[11]

Not only did France arm and train many of those who were later to carry out the killings, but there are allegations of French soldiers deliberately ignoring Tutsis who were about to be slaughtered, and forcing Tutsis out of refugee camps to be killed by *interahamwe*, as well as allegations that some French soldiers actually participated in the killing of Tutsis.

Alphonse Minyandinda is one of the few survivors of the Bisesero massacres in which *interahamwe* and Rwandan government army soldiers systematically fought and killed all but one thousand of forty to fifty thousand Tutsi who had banded together to defend themselves with sticks and stones. He is only now beginning to talk of his experiences there and says of the French soldiers

> We heard the good news that we were going to be saved and we came out from our hiding places and joined up with the French soldiers. They told us that our security was assured and that we did not have to worry about anything. It was a lie. The objective of the French soldiers was to gather us in order to make it easy for *interahamwe*

to exterminate those who remained. It seemed that French troops gave instructions to the *interahamwe* how to do their work. And the evidence of this, I am telling you, is that they were watching how the *interahamwe* were killing people. They did not do anything to stop them. At that time *interahamwe* killed the remnants and this was easy for them because we were encircled and could not flee. But if only the French soldiers did not say that they would protect us, many people would have stayed in hiding and survived those killings.

Many other countries, including the UK, the USA and Belgium, were to join the list of those who failed Rwanda in her hour of need. As Edmund Burke, the Irish-born politician and writer, said in a different situation: 'All that is necessary for the triumph of evil is for good men to do nothing.'

But in Rwanda the frightening rise of the militias was the more immediate concern. The *interahamwe* compiled the addresses of Tutsis and those lists were later used to identify and eliminate them. In schools, Tutsis and Hutus were separated to either side of the classroom. The organisation behind the genocide had already begun, and all over the country and repeatedly on the radio came the slogan *tuzabatsembatsemba* – 'We shall exterminate them.'

One of the other major reasons that ethnic hatred could fester so strongly in Rwandan society was the education of the youth. Young people were so dominant in the genocide that there was clearly a flaw in the educational system which allowed a generation to finish their schooling and still be convinced of their racial superiority. In many schools, Tutsis and Hutus were already separated before the genocide. Teachers talked in openly racial terms and the policies of Hutu power skewed the teaching population heavily in favour of Hutus, especially those with links to extremist groups. Justus Iyamuremye of the *Rwandan New Times* has written:

> the behaviour and the image portrayed by some of the adherents of the previous educational system is a true reflection of the type and personalities of their teachers and leaders, who sowed the seeds of hatred and discrimination. This therefore means that the 1994 Genocide was an eruption of accumulated hatred that had been implanted in the minds of the young generation, over a lengthy period of time. This is why people should understand analysts when they say that Genocide did not occur because of the death of the late President Juvenal Habyarimana but rather that it was a result of an ideology that had been deeply entrenched in the population.[12]

By early 1994 the intention by the Hutu extremists to destroy the Tutsi was unveiled. The culture of fear was complete and no one dared stand up against the extremist propaganda. One of the Hutu extremist leaders, Hassan Ngeze (convicted of incitement and conspiracy to commit genocide in December 2003 and jailed for life) made this statement in January 1994: 'We say to the *inyenzi* (cockroaches) that if they lift up their heads again it will no longer be necessary to fight the enemy in the bush. We will start by eliminating the internal enemy – they will disappear.'[13] The intention was to move from confronting the RPF army in the bush to eliminating the Tutsis inside the country. Tutsis were commonly called snakes or cockroaches, and the ideologists worked hard to dehumanise them completely. It would not be people that were being killed but cockroaches being chased and stamped down underfoot.

Dr Gregory Stanton of Genocide Watch has detailed eight stages that take place in most genocides.[14] The victims are classified, they are identified with negative symbolism, they are dehumanised, the perpetrators organise themselves, society is polarised between enemies and allies, the population is mobilised, extermination and 'purification' are undertaken, and then denial follows. By early 1994 in Rwanda, the first six stages had taken place.

During this time the United Nations sent in 2,165 peace-keepers and 321 military observers[15] under a 'chapter six' mandate, which is a peacekeeping mission and empowers the U.N. to help put an end to hostilities through diplomacy but without the use of force. It leaves little room for intervention if people begin to slaughter their neighbours.

After the killing had finished, many people were to ask why the United Nations did so little to stop the slaughter. One contributing factor was that the Rwandan situation came to boiling point just after the involvement of the United Nations in Bosnia and Somalia (where some American soldiers had been casualties), and there was little stomach in the corridors of power for intervention in another conflict. When the genocide began, very few world leaders made any positive move towards intervening and the United Nations, backed by major world leaders, forbade General Dallaire, commanding the United Nations' peacekeeping troops, from direct action to stop the killing. They even stopped him and his troops seizing known arms caches which were later to be used in the killing. The stage was set for the unleashing of horrific forces of brutality.

3

From Dusk to Darkness

On 6 April 1994, as dusk turned to darkness, President Habyarimana of Rwanda was returning from Dar es Salaam. He had been meeting with regional East African leaders who were putting pressure on him to move forward the efforts for peace, and was returning to Rwanda with the President of Burundi. As his plane approached Kigali airport it was shot down. People still disagree over who shot it down, whether it was Hutu extremists trying to sabotage peace efforts and initiate the genocide, the RPF trying to destabilise the country to provoke a war they could use to invade the rest of the country, or someone else.

What is clear is that the *interahamwe* and the Rwandan government army were well prepared for this event. Roadblocks and the shooting of Tutsis who were top of the lists began within one hour of the plane coming down. Hardline and extremist politicians suddenly disappeared from legislative and governmental duties to become involved in the co-ordination of the genocide and the Hutu moderates became very afraid – with good reason. Many were among the first to be targeted and killed, as political opposition was pre-emptively neutralised. In

the normally noisy, convivial streets of a Rwandan
evening Kigali fell silent, lights out, waiting for terror.

As the deep black of the African night turned to
dawn, government forces set out in armoured cars,
freshly unpacked assault rifles in hand. When the sun
rose over Kigali on 7 April, the genocide had already
begun. The *interahamwe* combined with the Presidential Guard, who were Rwanda's elite military force,
at the forefront of the killing. Where the *interahamwe*
met with resistance, the government soldiers or the
Presidential Guard, with their grenades and other
weaponry could be called on to break down the resistance of Tutsis trying to defend themselves. The
Rwandan government forces were soon to be involved
in the war against the RPF and were less virulent in
pursuing the genocide than the Presidential Guard, but
were nevertheless complicit in it. In addition, Rwanda
had a paramilitary police force called the *Gendarmerie*,
modelled on the French equivalent and consisting of
six thousand armed police. Like the army and Presidential Guard, it had increasingly excluded Tutsis and
was also part of the genocidal alliance, as were many
Hutus in the general population who were indoctrinated or coerced into taking up machetes, clubs and any
other killing implements, which included everything
from spears to agricultural hoes. They went from
house to house with lists of names, systematically
slaughtering then moving on.

With just over two thousand soldiers and an order not
to engage in conflict unless fired upon, the UN soldiers
listened helplessly to the screams and shots increasingly
heard through the city. Phone calls for help would be
suddenly interrupted by shooting and screaming and
the line would go dead. Roadblocks and *interahamwe*
night patrols to stop Tutsis escaping were set up through

the city. There was nowhere to run, nowhere to flee and no one to help.

Over the next hundred days, those cries would echo round the world with no answer. Even after hundreds of thousands of Rwandans lay slaughtered in churches, streets and fields, and after numerous communications from their own forces in the country detailing the scale of the killing, and despite their own Secretary General describing the killing publicly as genocide, the response of the United Nations Security Council on 1 July was to establish a 'Commission of Experts' to investigate 'possible acts of genocide.'[16] The United States prevented an attempt to say 'genocide has occurred' as late as 16 May.[17] If ever there was less need for a committee and more need for action, it was then. Wary of possible casualties, the UN had already reduced its force from a peak of 2,165 to 444 by early May. Typical of the desperation of Rwandans in those days are the words of nine-year-old Nadia Uwimbabazi, who was trying to find a safe place to shelter after her family was killed: 'On the following day we fled and went to a technical school at Kicukiro [featured in the film *Shooting Dogs*] because we had learned that many other people had gone there and there was a United Nations force that camped there. The UN forces had already gone and we saw that many hundreds or thousands had been killed there.' Although the UN must shoulder the blame for its own inadequate response, member countries themselves did not respond well to requests for soldiers, logistical support and finance.

However, although the UN and the national governments in the democratic world continued to obstruct any serious attempt to stop the slaughter, democratic governments tend to respond to public demand and the public demanded very little. In the later weeks of the

genocide, the clamour for more coverage of the murder
of the ex-wife of former football star turned media
celebrity O J Simpson drowned out the cries of a
Rwandan genocide and the slaughter of a million
Africans. Governments should not shoulder the whole
blame for our lack of action: they are the people's repre-
sentatives, and the UN is only as good as its member
countries make it. The truth is that a million African
lives were not worth very much to the western world.

For Patricia* and her five brothers and sisters, what
followed was typical of the desperate struggle for Tutsi
families to survive. As the burning and killing began, the
family fled into the woods. Pursued into their hiding
places, the family was attacked, and her parents and
brothers clubbed and hacked to death. Patricia and her
three sisters escaped but their house was burnt to the
ground. They walked for ten hours to their grandparents'
home but found it also burnt out. They discovered their
grandparents hiding in bushes nearby and hid through
the night on the hillside. In the morning they were discovered. The grandfather was killed but the girls escaped
again. Bewildered and helpless, they walked back again
to their home area. On the way they met a family friend
– a Hutu man who took them to his home. Once there,
they were threatened with death and, as Patricia
explains: 'We started to be employed as slaves.'

Shortly afterwards, at fifteen years old, Patricia was
told she would be married that night. They fled to hide
in the bushes again, spending four days and nights
without food, drinking rainwater and shivering through
the wet nights. Driven out of hiding by hunger and
thirst, they emerged from the bushes and were caught at
a roadblock. There Patricia was bought for five hundred
Rwandan francs (about 75 pence then) by an *interahamwe*, and held captive by him. The sisters fled and

were reunited with Patricia after she was eventually rescued by the RPF.

When the country was liberated, Patricia and her sisters walked for three days to a displaced people's camp. Patricia cared for her sisters until they found an aunt who took them in. However, the aunt's husband raped Patricia's sister Donathe,* and shortly afterwards he died of AIDS. Now left homeless, the aunt rented a one-room house with Patricia and her three sisters. Shortly afterwards a baby was born to Donathe from the rape. With another young child joining them, there were now seven in the family, living in a room about fifteen feet by ten. Three of them had to sleep in a nearby church in the red-light district every night.

Such was the future for multitudes of children. The work of exterminating the Tutsi 'cockroaches' had started to litter the streets of Kigali with bodies. The extremist radio station RTLM (*Radio Télévision Libre de Mille Collines* – Independent Radio Television of a Thousand Hills) soon became the only radio station on air and began to broadcast calls for its listeners to go out and kill the Tutsis. During the three months of slaughter, it would give details of Tutsis who were still alive and exhort the listeners to finish killing them, as well as any Hutus who did not hate Tutsis. This pressure on Hutus to show hatred for Tutsis became a key element in the fear that drove many of them to kill. Many Hutus without their identity cards were forced to prove their ethnic origin by killing captured Tutsis or being killed themselves.

When the genocide began, the war between the Rwandan Patriotic Front (RPF) and the government forces also restarted. The RPF was in the north of the country, with a contingent of six hundred holed up in Kigali as part of an interim peace agreement. Part of the

RPF force was sent to buttress the contingent in Kigali while the main force pushed down the east side of Rwanda and swung round west to the south of Kigali. By the end of May they occupied most of the eastern half of Rwanda and, within three months, they had overwhelmed the less motivated and sometimes blood- and alcohol-drunk government soldiers and *interahamwe*, and begun a final assault on the capital. During those three months, RPF soldiers in the capital continued to battle with government forces and, as the RPF surrounded the city, resistance crumbled and it fell on 4 July. Government officials and *genocidaires* fled like snow off a dyke, and suddenly the noise of shellfire and guns gave way to silence.

Mopping-up operations continued in the west and north-west of the country, with the last government stronghold taken on 17 July. On 19 July, 1994, the RPF established the Government of National Unity with four other political parties: the Liberal Party (PL), the Social Democratic Party (PSD), the Christian Democratic Party (PDC) and the Republican Democratic Movement (MDR).

Before the end of the war, an area in the south-west of the country was still occupied by government forces, and the French government succeeded in getting a force of French soldiers into this area with 'Operation Turquoise': the area became known as the 'Turquoise Zone.' In the final days of the killing, news of this intervention reached the ears of the *genocidaires* and, convinced of the complicity of the new forces, they realised they could act with impunity – not only in the Turquoise Zone but elsewhere. The *genocidaires* therefore made a renewed effort to exterminate survivors.

Estimates vary, but about 75-80 per cent of the Tutsi population was killed, and 2 per cent of the Hutu population (some killed as moderates and some by RPF soldiers in revenge or summary executions).[18] Children and babies were exterminated to prevent a new generation of Tutsis surviving, but estimates of between one hundred and three hundred thousand orphans are common. Over two million people fled to Congo, Burundi and Tanzania, with a quarter of a million crossing one border point in south-east Rwanda in twenty-four hours – the fastest and largest movement of displaced people ever known. These were mainly Hutus fleeing from the RPF, as most Tutsis did not get through road blocks and so could not flee. Large areas of Rwanda were left virtually deserted.

Many of the *interahamwe* fled to refugee camps during the genocide, fearful of attacks from RPF soldiers. In the camps they organised themselves back into their district, sector and cell systems, and continued to rape and kill Tutsis. About fifteen thousand Congolese Tutsis in the areas bordering Rwanda were also ethnically cleansed by those *interahamwe*. By the end of the genocide the RPF had taken power and RPF soldiers had crossed the border into the Congo to tackle the *interahamwe* before they re-entered Rwanda. In the meantime, about fifty thousand people had died of cholera in the camps. When the genocide ended, there were three million internally displaced people, most seeking refuge in the French 'Turquoise Zone' in the south-west; two million refugees, mainly in what was then Zaire and Tanzania; and one million dead, out of a population of about seven and a half million.

4

Past Revival – Future Hope

It is out of this chaos that Rwanda is rebuilding. The country is not covering up its past, but bravely facing its true magnitude with the words 'Never Again' emblazoned upon its numerous memorials. As God's people, Christians have a great responsibility and privilege to be at the forefront of the rebuilding of the nation, and to forge love and unity through the power of the cross. One of the country's Christian MPs, Mukamurangwa Sebera Harriett, told me one day while travelling together in Rwanda: 'After the genocide we are very sure the country is now blessed.' It is a remarkable statement of hope, but it is borne out by the testimonies of God's power to restore broken lives and unite divided hearts.

The church in Rwanda has historically been dominated by the Roman Catholic Church, introduced in 1900 by Cardinal Lavigerie and the 'White Fathers' from Germany and later promoted by the Belgian colonists. German Lutherans and Belgian Reformed Protestants started missions in 1907, and 'Ruanda Mission' evangelists entered the country in 1922. The Ruanda Mission was part of the Church Missionary Society and the Anglican Church grew out of its work. Baptist churches were also established in the 1920s. Shortly before the genocide, in a census in 1991, 63 per cent of Rwandans considered themselves Roman Catholic, 19 per cent Protestant, and 8 per cent Seventh Day Adventist.

Jay Carney of the Catholic University of America points out that the 'White Fathers' top-down evangelisation approach often led them to seek a place at the centre of political power rather than the prophetic margins. It was Catholic Church policy to focus efforts on converting those in authority, in the hope that the people under them would follow suit. Throughout the history of the Catholic Church in Rwanda the alliance between the church, royalty and political rule has led to difficulties in maintaining the mission as a religious and not a political endeavour.

In the late 1950s some more forward-thinking priests became concerned for the exploited underdog status of the Hutus, although they managed to direct the blame for this onto the Tutsi ruling class rather than the colonial architects of the hardened tribal system. This movement for Hutu emancipation by a minority of priests coincided with the rise of a Rwandan independence movement championed by the Tutsi ruling class, and led to the Roman Catholic Church rapidly shifting its support from the Tutsis to the growing Hutu superiority movement. By 1962, with the help of the church, the new government was completely Hutu-dominated. Grégoire Kayibanda, the first President of the fledgling independent Rwanda in 1962, had served as editor of the Catholic newspaper *Kinyamateka*. The Catholic Church sent him to Europe for training, and many other Hutu politicians at independence were church employees or had been educated and promoted out of Catholic seminaries.

Kayibanda was deposed in 1973 and replaced by Habyarimana, who considered himself a strong

Catholic. His *Mouvement Révolutionnaire National pour le
Développement* (MRND) party became the only political
party in Rwanda for the next twenty-seven years, and
continued the close alliance between church and state. It
is clear therefore that the crucial time for the church
came a long time before 1994. By then, many decades of
collusion between church and politics seemed to have
robbed the church of its conscience. There were notable
exceptions: Catholic bishops of Kabgayi and Nyundo
wrote and spoke denouncing the training of civilian
militias and the distribution of arms to civilians. It must
also be said that some pastors, priests and nuns acted
with great bravery and integrity, and 106 Catholic
priests and 250 nuns were killed during the genocide,
including some Tutsi clergy killed by their own flocks.
But the general alignment with a corrupt and oppressive
regime reaped devastating consequences, and the
Catholic Church was deeply compromised as many
priests and nuns were in cahoots with the *interahamwe*.
Mahmood Mamdani, Director of African Studies and
Professor of Government at Columbia University, USA,
asserts that 'the Church was the womb that nurtured the
leadership of the insurgent Hutu movement.'

The Protestant churches were not as closely linked to
the political elite as the Catholic Church, and though
some Protestant clergy were involved in facilitating
genocide, there were fewer incidents of direct collusion
with the *genocidaires* among them. However, they did
not speak with a clear voice against the ethnic division,
and with about twenty per cent of the population being
members of their churches, the opportunity to exert a
strong restraint on the killing was not taken.

The East African revival must be seen as the background to the Rwandan genocide. Amongst those desperately seeking for renewal in the church in the late

1920s was an English missionary from the Ruanda Mission, Joe Church, and a Ugandan, Simeoni Nsibambi. They met in their spiritual hunger at Kampala where Joe Church was resting, exhausted after a famine that had led to many deaths and great distress. The two men discovered in each other the same passionate desire for revival, and resolved before God to live a life of sanctification and Spirit fullness. They were soon joined by Simeoni's brother Blasio Kigozi, and the expanding group became known as the *abaka* – the men of fire. Throughout the early 1930s, they ceaselessly criss-crossed Rwanda, preaching the gospel and calling for deeper holiness and Spirit fullness. Those who responded sought to live in complete openness and honesty before each other, frequently weeping in repentance, devouring the word and spending much time in prayer, often rising by 4.00 a.m. to spend two hours in prayer before the day's work began. At that time women, especially those considered as higher-class, were often confined to their huts and the small piece of land surrounding it, the *rugo*, but women who were set on fire by God could not be constrained any longer and joined the itinerant preaching and praising.

Blasio Kigozi played a pivotal part in leading a ten-day Anglican revival convention in Kabale, Uganda, and there were signs of a rising tide of the Spirit's power. Shortly afterwards Kigozi contracted a severe fever and died suddenly in hospital crying *Zuzaka! Zuzaka!* (Awake! Awake!), the word that was soon to be inscribed on his gravestone.

At the end of June 1936 the mission station and hospital at Gahini, which had been at the centre of much that had gone on among those touched by the revival, was the centre of an even stronger breakthrough. It began with the girls of the mission school, who were seeking God in prayer when a deep consciousness of sin broke out and they began to weep and cry. Some non-Christian girls had come to disturb the meeting and seek contact with ancestral spirits; the spiritual battle was intense, and there were loud cries and screams as the girls appeared to be wrestling the powers of darkness. God broke through among them, and at the same time from various other parts of the mission station singing and crying began as many were smitten by the power of the Spirit.

In the days that followed the mission station was marked by great conviction of sin leading to deep repentance, a devotion to prayer and a hunger for the word, and the revival began to spread. Rapidly it reached Burundi, Uganda and Congo, and then Tanzania and Kenya. The believers were nicknamed *Balokole* – the saved ones. The revival was not a short-term, localised phenomenon, but widened and spread for decades throughout East Africa. Although some churches grew cold and the revival changed shape in different regions, the evangelical thrust of the gospel continued to touch large areas of east and central Africa. As time went by the evangelical thrust was maintained, but the emphasis on changed lives diminished. The message of salvation was repeatedly shouted by the preacher, but the necessary discipleship and Christian teaching were not so evident.

In the early years of the revival the Europeans and Africans experienced a wonderful unity. The teams that travelled throughout Rwanda proclaiming the gospel were often mixed, and preached a message that spoke clearly of level ground among all people at the foot of the cross. There was not always such unity between those who supported the revival and those who did not, and the latter were often unhappy with its strong emotions and manifestations, but God continued to teach his people lessons of humility and forbearance.

Despite the glory of the revival it did not penetrate society as a whole. Thousands were saved (an estimated twenty thousand through the revival meetings by 1942) and there was a fire in the bellies of the believers, but those involved in the revival were not embraced by Rwandan society which remained nominally Christian, mainly Catholic, but largely unmoved.

By 1994 the political mechanisms exercising control over the population were deeply entrenched, which meant that most positions of power in sectors such as politics, education, local government and the judiciary belonged to those who were sympathetic to or supportive of the government's racial propaganda. It must be remembered that over twenty-eight thousand leaders at various levels of national and local government have been implicated in the genocide.[19] The ideology of ethnic cleansing had also pervaded the nation through the media. By 1994 any dissenting voice would be that of a martyr, and it would be too late to stop the inevitable.

When the genocide broke out, the *interahamwe* quickly revealed itself to be a highly organised, well-oiled killing machine. One of its chief tactics was to strike so much fear into the population that normal citizens became killers of their own neighbours, relatives and sometimes even family. The word *interahamwe*, as mentioned earlier, is taken from *gutera* which has various meanings including 'to attack'. A related word is *igitero*[20] which signifies a group of people who have come together to wage war or attack others. Once members of the *interahamwe* had formed killing mobs, usually of twenty to a hundred people, they would coerce others into becoming involved. Sometimes an *igitero* would grow to become thousands strong when an attack on a large group of

Tutsis was planned. When confronted with an *igitero*
packed with angry, weapon-wielding *interahamwe* insisting they take part in the killing, it was difficult for anyone to maintain integrity and resist. Other ordinary
citizens did join the *ibitero* (plural) and take part in the
killing out of spite, jealousy or in order to steal the victims' belongings, but many others were compelled by
fear.

By this time the ability of the church to cry out against
the intimidation and violence had been seriously compromised, and individuals were left to maintain a stand
for truth without a serious attempt by the church to create
a united front against the violence and killing. When the
church allows itself to be moulded by the world it cannot
change shape easily. It had been pressed into conformity
with ungodly thinking, and found itself too bound to
break free in time to stop the onrushing tragedy.

When genocide broke out, the level of fear undoubt-
edly led some born-again Christians to be coerced into
the killing. Others, however, acted with incredible bravery. At a number of places, including Muhima, Kigali
and Rugarika, Christians who were praying were called
to divide into Tutsis and Hutus and refused to do so,
choosing to die together instead.

There are some Christians in Rwanda who believe
that God, though not responsible for or willing the genocide, did not prevent it because of the weakness of the
church and its need for cleansing. What is clear is that
the church has been made vividly aware of its need to
awaken and deal with its nominalism and shallowness.
It is also clear that God has been exceptionally gracious
in his dealings with the church in the post-genocide
years. The words of Emmanuel Kolini, who was inaugu-
rated as the new Archbishop of the Anglican church of
Rwanda in 1997, deserve to be repeated:

When I hear stories from women, men and children I wonder why Rwandans laugh and look smart. There is only one answer – we have plenty of grace – that's how we can laugh, otherwise we should be mourning, in tears or hang ourselves. What happened in Rwanda is beyond understanding and imagination but we are experiencing the grace of God. A journalist wrote that the angels left Rwanda – yes in a sense – but it is not true. God was present and God is with us . . . I think this is a second move of the church of Rwanda. It is my prayer that genocide turn into blessing, not only for Rwanda but for the entire world. Rwanda has been a challenge to Christianity, it's a challenge to us. We didn't witness our love and truth. It's time. Jesus has to be glorified. The Church has an answer, by grace, by obedience. I don't believe in political salvation, I believe in biblical salvation. That's why I take the church as responsible for the healing, for the construction, for the spiritual revival of Rwanda and East Africa.[21]

In December 1996 a number of Rwandans living abroad as well as many from Rwanda, met in Detmold, Germany to pray and to discuss the aftermath of the genocide. God broke into the meeting, and confession and repentance led to them drawing up a document called the Detmold Confession. Inspired by Ezekiel 22:30 which talks of standing in the gap, the participants and others who were encouraged to join the process, including some prominent church leaders, felt called by God to take on the crimes and shortcomings of their respective groups and confess them before God. The spirit of the document is vividly caught in the following excerpts:

The Rwandan people will never be reconciled with each other unless each party agrees to kneel down before the

suffering of the other party, to confess their own offence
and to humbly ask forgiveness of their victims . . . therefore we Hutu Christians, present at Detmold, recognise
our group has oppressed the Tutsi in various ways since
1959. We confess the massacres at different periods, cul-
minating in the genocide of 1994. We are ashamed of the
horrors and atrocities . . . we carry the weight of this
unspeakable crime and accept to bear the consequences
without resentment. We humbly implore forgiveness of
God and our Tutsi brothers and sisters for all the evil we
have inflicted on them. We commit ourselves to do
whatever we can to restore their honour and dignity and
to regain our lost humanity in their eyes. . . .

We Tutsi also implore God and our Hutu brothers and sisters for forgiveness for certain arrogant and contemptu-
ous attitudes shown to them throughout our history in the
name of a ridiculous complex of ethnic superiority. . . .

We western Christians, present at Detmold, confess that
since the first arrival of the Europeans in Rwanda, we
have seriously contributed to the increase of divisions in
the Rwanda people. We regret that feeling too sure of
our superiority we discriminated between people by
generalising and judging some as good and others as
bad. We regret that our countries have contributed to
violence by delivering arms . . . we also regret our silence
and our abandon of the Rwanda people during the genocide and massacres of 1994. For all this harm, we implore
God and our Rwandan brothers and sisters to forgive us
for not respecting them as they are and we want to commit ourselves with Jesus to a path of listening and soli-
darity . . . we thank the Father, who has given us His
spirit to 'break our hearts of stone' and to free us from
the mistrust and fear which separated us. He has remade

us brothers and sisters committed to the Way of His Son, who died and rose again to reconcile man to God and to one another.[22]

The grace of God has continued to renew significant portions of the church, both in some mainstream denominations and in the growing non-mainstream churches. At the end of the millennium a National Prayer Conference was organised by many of those churches and Christian organisations in a wonderful spirit of unity. On the last day of 1999, fifteen thousand Rwandans committed themselves to truly worship God and work for his glory in the nation. On that day, two passages from the word of God dominated the prayer times. The first was 2 Chronicles 7:13-15, and the Spirit of God moved those praying to confess, repent and humble themselves before God. A spirit of contrition and repentance was moving among the people as they cried to God for forgiveness, for personal and collective sin. As Hutus repented for the bloodstains on their hands of almost four decades and asked forgiveness from God and from the Tutsis, the Tutsis also repented of their hatred, resentment and spirit of revenge, and asked forgiveness.

The other passage was Psalm 85, which is truly the cry of the church during the years following the genocide as God continues to renew, cleanse and use his people. It captures so beautifully and powerfully the heart of God's people calling on their God

O Lord, You showed favour to your land;
You restored the captivity of Jacob.
You forgave the iniquity of Your people;
You covered all their sin. . . .
Restore us, O God of our salvation,

And cause Your indignation toward us to cease. . . .
Will You not Yourself revive us again that Your people
may rejoice in You?
. . . Lovingkindness and truth have met together,
Righteousness and peace have kissed each other. . . .
Indeed the Lord will give what is good,
And our land will yield its produce.

5

The Road to Healing

It is New Years' Eve 2005. The widows and orphans of Solace Ministries (a Rwandan Christian organisation reaching out to survivors of the genocide and led by a survivor, Jean Gakwandi), are having a Christmas and New Year celebration. There is worship and testimony and choirs and preaching and food. The sun beats down through a slightly hazy blue sky, but there are some tents erected to provide shelter. Droscella, who is leading the service, had been married for one month when the genocide came and she was widowed, but after the healing of God touched her life she is now strong in the Lord and helping others to find healing in Christ. The girl leading the choir is Constantine, the only survivor of her family, who worships with fervour and passion. Like everything else involving widows and orphans in Rwanda the reality of the genocide cannot be sidelined, but it is faced and overcome through the bravery and faith of these widows and orphans. The drums are pounded with home-made drumsticks made from branches and the castanets round the dancers' feet clash with amazing precision as their feet stamp and shuffle on the dusty soil. Someone reads a poem about Jesus, the Lord of peace, bringing peace to Rwandan hearts.

It is a big day for Beatrice.* For eleven years she pushed the pain down, unable to face the terrors of her ordeal. Emotionless and numb, empty and hopeless, she stumbled through the long days wondering why she survived. But over the last months she has come to Solace ministries and found a place to face the past and begin a new future. Today she is talking about what she went through and the hope she now has. It is the first time she has talked publicly of her ordeal. I have heard it said in Rwanda that 'the greatest gift you can give to a hurting person is to listen to them.' There are well over six hundred people listening to Beatrice at this Christmas celebration. She starts by giving thanks.

'I want to first thank Solace for comforting us. We were sad, abandoned and scattered. I want to thank God for this day so that we can come together and thank God. I do not want to continue repeating this, but we say this so that those who do not know can understand.'

Beatrice is not as slim as many Rwandans but her face is pretty with straight dark hair, and she is dressed attractively in a bright blue Rwandan dress with a black and red top. Her reference to wanting others to know and understand the trauma of Rwanda is frequently and insistently repeated among the survivors of the genocide. She begins her story.

'On 7 April I was in a place called Gatenga.' Gatenga is a poorer area in the east of the capital Kigali.

> What I saw after the President's plane crashed was very terrible. In the morning the *interahamwe* surrounded our house. I was at home with the children and some others, and my husband was in a neighbouring house discussing what had happened. They started shooting into the house. One of them said, 'Stop – let's look for the husband.' My husband had to stay away because of this

and in the evening they came back and drove us out of the house. I and my children were taken to the leader's house who asked where my husband was. I told them I didn't know but he said, 'I have killed him and will make you my second wife. I have also killed all your friends and relatives.'

However, my husband was not yet dead but had been discovered in a neighbouring house and was brought in tied up. The neighbours had all been killed. My husband was then beaten very hard in front of me to make him tell where other Tutsis were. I was also being tortured. Then six men raped me in front of my husband. I was kept there like this for a week and then they took us back to our house and started shooting at us. My elder child ran away but I had a baby who was breastfeeding and another on my back. Both of them and my husband were killed.

Beatrice was spared to be the wife of the killer of her husband and children. Now she is weeping and being comforted by one of the Solace widows who has great compassion and strength for such times. She continues to speak, determined to bring the whole event to light. She knows that the bondage of fear must be broken, and the shame and guilt faced and removed. Her weeping intensifies as she faces the nightmare that followed.

'I was the only one who remained alive but I was very wounded. I could not do anything and I was weak because they did not let me eat or drink. They shot my family at 4.00 p.m. and there was a lot of blood. I was very thirsty and started licking the blood.'

She is sobbing intensely. Throughout the testimony, outbursts of support and sighs of pain have accompanied her words. The widows here know what it's like. But now a woman begins to scream. She screams and screams. Saliva pours from her mouth and her hands are clamped over her ears. She is supported by two women helpers, as her legs have folded underneath her. She is helped out of the meeting, screaming, dripping saliva and covering her ears. Beatrice moves to a close.

'I cannot tell you everything that happened. Sometimes I cannot sleep because of the pain from my injuries. But I am very grateful that Solace has helped me and I want to thank them for all they have done.'

It is a triumph for Beatrice. She is making progress. Not only is the hidden past being faced, but she has found faith in Christ and is beginning to discover a hope and a future. She is now receiving counselling and consistent prayer. The demonic power of her ordeal has been broken, and every week brings further progress. She is learning to lay the burden of her pain, her shame and her guilt at the cross and now wants to live, which is one of the major turning points for women who have been through such ordeals. And now she joins other widows and orphans who meet regularly to worship and pray and support each other. She has also started to become involved in teaching other widows and the heads of child-led households how to embroider and crochet and earn a living. She works patiently, watching over their work, teaching, encouraging and building a future for them. She herself is being helped to market and sell the products. Droscella, one of the helpers at Solace, remarks: 'When you see her you wouldn't imagine what happened to her.' When she sits with her group of apprentice embroiderers there is a peace upon her, and the expressionless eyes of the hopeless have left. She smiles with an open face and thanks God for the progress she is making.

For Julienne,* who was carried out, the process is just beginning. Julienne has come to some meetings before but never faced her own ordeal. One of the first signs of the depth of the trauma suffered by the survivors is the absence of emotion. So terrible was the trauma that survivors were instantly and completely numbed. Children would show no emotion when they found their parents had been killed, and wives would not cry or mourn for their husbands. But the eyes would retreat into a far distant look and their souls would seem as dead as the bodies of their beloved. Like the molten lava that boils deep down under the volcanoes in northern Rwanda, the pain and trauma have nowhere to go and the pressure keeps building.

Julienne is comforted and calmed and rejoins the meeting. A young woman called Kabatesi helps her; an orphan and head of her family now. The years of desperately seeking for enough food have taken their toll on Kabatesi, and her body is thin and fragile. She was deeply traumatised during the genocide at the age of nine. Her mother and father and seven brothers and sisters were killed. She looks after her sick brother who is dying with AIDS and has lost his sanity as a result, as well as her younger surviving sister. The younger sister was on her mother's back when the mother was killed, and was badly beaten and injured. When Kabatesi first came to Solace not so long ago she would talk non-stop for more than three hours. With counselling and prayer she is a new person, her rapid shocked ramblings replaced by a new peace and strength, and she speaks with grace and wisdom.

She sacrificed her school education in order to care for her sister and her niece in addition to her brother, feeding them and paying the rent. The home was a broken-down mud shack and they were nicknamed 'the children of the broken-down home.' In 2003 they were thrown out of that shelter and Kabatesi sat on the dusty street crying as her permanent headache pounded on. 'Does God really know me?' she cried. 'Does he think I am just an inanimate stone to be ignored?' After coming to Solace in 2003, because of her extreme difficulties they purchased a small house for her in Kigali. She could not believe it: 'It is really a miracle,' she said. 'I have found a family here and been taken in as a daughter.' Although she is slightly built, she has a courageous heart and, despite its bare mud walls, her home has the warm atmosphere of a place of hope. Today she is ministering comfort to Julienne and starting to sow her own healing into others.

The next day Julienne returns and begins to be counselled. She grasps eagerly the opportunity to share what has happened to her, as she feels the love of Christ and the support of many loving hearts around her. She had tried to escape south to Burundi, but could not get over the border without being detected and had to hide in the marshes. There were many bodies floating around her. Surrounded by *interahamwe* and unable to leave the marsh for two weeks, she was forced to drink water mixed with blood from the bodies. Her distress was intensified when she saw her own mother's body floating past. All this had been buried deep inside, but the mention of drinking blood had finally broken the dam. On the first day of the year, Julienne receives her first counselling, exposes the pain inside and begins the long road to recovery, almost twelve years after she first went numb.

This is why there is such emphasis on testifying to the reality of suffering in Rwanda. To have your pain validated by others who can support and encourage you is the first vital step to healing. It allows the light into the darkness and identifies the burden that needs to be laid at the cross. Like a giant abscess of the soul being pierced, the enemy's poison can now be drawn off. The testimonies of these widows and orphans have been dearly paid for. As I listen to Beatrice, the tears are not only for her pain, but for her brave fight to overcome the devil and find a hope, a future and a life worth living – a life rising from the ashes of her destroyed life. There are many widows in Rwanda who will admit there is a future for the next generation. They see the efforts at peace and reconciliation of the ethnic groups and they see some progress in Rwanda's governance and infrastructure. But too often the words are the same: 'There is hope for my children and grandchildren, but my life finished in 1994.' For Beatrice and Julienne, their lives are beginning again, one further on than the other, but those who are counselling and praying with them are confident that both will be healed through the love of God displayed on the cross.

There is one more testimony today. Donatilla Gahongayire was ten when the genocide began and she went through what no ten-year-old should ever have to bear. She is wearing a bright yellow dress and touches her nose slightly nervously as she starts to speak. Mama Lambert, a wonderful woman with a strong caring spirit, is standing at her shoulder, supporting and encouraging. Brought up to sing and worship and pray three times a day by a Catholic father and Protestant mother, Donatilla had a family full of love and happiness. The night the genocide began she was at home in the area of Kigali known as Kimironko, which faces the hill of Kanombe on which the airport is perched. She heard the President's plane crash, and innocently thought the President would be buried and life would carry on as normal. How little of the fomenting hatred those young children understood in the days before the genocide.

The next morning there was a commotion outside and a group of youths surrounded the house and began to break in. For a moment Donatilla was relieved when she saw a young man to whom her father was godfather. She presumed he had come to rescue them, but his intentions became clear: 'Everything we had as friends before is finished,' he barked, and joined the rest of the group in forcing them out. The family were lined up outside the house, father, mother and five children.

She remembers how they started to slash and chop at her helpless parents with machetes and begins to weep quietly as she shares her story. The orphans and widows listen intently, silently praying for more strength for her to unburden the horror, and willing her on. Suddenly, she tells them, she saw her father's body slumped on the ground and his head rolling away from it. It was an awful sight that has embedded itself in her thoughts and nightmares.

Immediately the killers turned to her mother and slashed her to death, then her older brother fell dead under the onslaught of machetes and clubs. The killing stopped while her sister was taken and brutally raped. She would later die from her injuries. When the rape was finished, Donatilla was taken with her two other siblings to a nearby camp where people were held captive, and she was beaten and raped with her other sister. The killers' taunts that the Tutsis' God was dead seemed all too real to her as her childhood faith and joy disappeared.

She managed to find a way to leave the camp, and made for her grandmother's home. After walking for three days with a child strapped to her back, she arrived to find there were only dead and dying bodies, their houses looted and destroyed. Her grandmother was one of the dying and was in too bad a shape to survive. Like so many others, Donatilla was left alone in the world, with no one to turn to, nowhere to go, and only the company of nightmares and fear. There was nothing to eat and she wandered pointlessly back towards Kigali, all the time carrying her bundle of a baby sister on her back. Mile after mile she walked with her back aching, her legs protesting, but her young sister's cries steadily reduced to a whimper. At last she found a group of Tutsis gathered together, huddled into a defenceless crowd for supposed protection. A woman kindly helped her unburden her sister from her back, but as Donatilla relieved herself of her precious cargo, she was stunned and shattered again. Donatilla was faced with a dead sister: she had been carrying her exhausted, dehydrated and famished body all the way to death.

Suddenly the group was attacked, and the illusion of protection instantly vanished with the onslaught of slashing *interahamwe*. Donatilla was forced to run for her life, leaving her dead baby sister on the ground. She barely had time to realise she had died, and later had to deal with the false but haunting thought that she might have still been alive. She escaped, and a few days later fell into the hands of the advancing RPF army and was safe. At the time, what she saw led her to conclude: 'There is no God.'

'But now I believe God was directing me and keeping me safe,' she insists, 'though I still had much to go through.' Two sisters survived, both beaten and raped, with one of them made pregnant. In the months and years that followed the trauma continued to worsen: 'I found I was also pregnant because of the rape,' Donatilla continues, 'and later on my sisters both died from their rape injuries and AIDS. I tried suicide three times and life was very hard. I hated God. I could not understand how he could let me suffer this much.'

'On 8 June 2003 I went to church, but it was to waste my time.' But she found something there that wasn't a waste of her time. 'There the pastor preached on

Matthew 6:31: "So do not worry, saying what shall we eat, or what shall we drink, or what shall we wear?" I came to the conclusion that it was God who fed us, who gave us clothes, and who protected us in the night. And I realised that he loved us very much. I repented of my sins and renewed my relationship with God.'

The trauma didn't disappear overnight and sometimes her faith has taken a heavy battering. In 2004 she arrived at Solace still deeply traumatised, but over the months that followed the healing progressed and her life took on meaning and value. 'I became a child again,' she says. She started to find healing through the love and prayers of the helpers and survivors there. 'I put my burden down and I got a new family, Jean Gakwandi as my father, and I got other sisters and brothers, uncles, aunts, grandfather and grandmother, cousins and so on.' As she shares her story she talks calmly, occasionally composing herself but never losing her peace in God. She wants to finish with a poem of gratitude to God for Solace; the names in the poem are of those who work there.

> Oh Solace, when I am determined to thank you, it is
> When I am praying,
> Beyond my wildest thoughts,
> For you permitted me to continue to live.
> As the enemy had a plan to persecute me
> To take away the branches and make the tree dry
> You have been a hero for me.
>
> Continue to support me in my life
> That my anxieties may end
> And my sorrows be forgotten,
> And that I live free of my enemies and problems.
> You always feed me –

Discipline me if I become extravagant,
Because God will always protect me.
I implore you to show me my mistakes.

And He told you: 'I will give you my resources
And I will multiply them and call you welcome.'
Those who join you will be welcome
For they will join Me there.
Solace, let me pray for you, that you have many
Supporters, many more parents who remind us that
A child should be blessed with an education.
May you have more heroes.

May we always be welcomed by Denise and Consolee.
They are full of compassion.
May we be joyfully received by Beata and Daphrose
Who will look after us as if they were our aunts
And will know our hearts' needs.

You are the first one I pray for,
And the church He gave us is the
One you followed,
The one that comforts and
Supports orphans and widows.

The One who gave you to me
Is the Almighty God.
When I was struggling, I turned
My eyes to God alone
And He who made the ears heard me.
My determination is to thank you
For He gave me to you and you
Obeyed His will.
May you always have Gakwandi
Who loved, heard and comforted me.

May you always have Kayumba,
Who swore not to sleep while
Others could not sleep.

We, your orphans, are thankful.
We don't have any cattle,
We don't have any fields,
But we are cherished by our God
And on the day we receive our reward
The merit will be yours.

These three survivors, Beatrice, Julienne and Donatilla, are all at different stages in the healing process. Their journeys to find comfort and hope in Christ have begun at different times, in different ways and at different speeds. But they have found the road to healing and are going in the right direction. There are many hurdles on the road – the pain of losing loved ones, the trauma and nightmares, the stigma and horror of rape, forgiveness and reconciliation, learning to trust and build healthy relationships, renewing shattered faith, and problems of education, health and work.

As Donatilla's testimony finishes, her friend Mucyo leads the youth in a song. It is in *Kinyarwandan*, but the tune is known worldwide.

Father God, I wonder
how I managed to exist
without the knowledge of your parenthood
and your loving care.
But now I am your child,
I am adopted in your family,
and I will never be alone,
for Father God you're there beside me.

Ian Smale Copyright (c) 1984 Thankyou Music[23]

6

Forgiving the Unforgivable

To forgive is to release two sets of chains – those by which we would seek to bind the offender in guilt, and those by which we bind ourselves in bitterness. Bitterness is simply unforgiveness that expresses itself through anger. When injustice is as extreme as in Rwanda, where innocence and helplessness counted for nothing to those who killed, forgiveness is not easy. One day whilst eating lunch at a church, my wife Izzy and I were served by Zula.* Her story was aching in its tragedy: buried under piles of bodies with only her head and neck free, she watched her husband and son being killed, and was eventually pulled free to find her baby at her breast crushed to death. The next day Izzy was preaching on forgiveness and down to the front of the church came Zula, releasing her burden of unforgiveness and letting the cool breeze of God's healing power blow over the hot tears she shed. How inadequate we felt to pray for this dear young woman, how trite can words seem and how empty was the message on forgiveness without the love of the cross to fill the aching voids of her heart. But God broke the chains, and Zula is free to dance and sing as she worships God. Forgiveness is not an easy journey, but its destination is triumph and freedom.

In a fascinating piece of writing entitled *Forgiveness and Reconciliation*, Duncan Morrow reminds the reader that 'we speak of forgiveness far too cheaply. By always talking about the noun – forgiveness – we easily give the impression that this is a readily accessible, ready-to-wear object, with a predictable shape. Yet forgiveness is nothing more nor less than the result of forgiving: it takes all of its meaning from an active verb.'[24]

Forgiveness always involves the injured person taking a risk, paying a price, and releasing a debt. Those who have the greatest debt to release pay the highest price, and the rest of us can only wonder at such grace. For those in Rwanda who still suffer from deep trauma as a result of their experiences, it takes deep courage to release the debtor while they pay a heavy price themselves.

The *Gacaca* (local courts where those suspected of genocidal acts or collaboration have to reveal and confess the extent and details of their involvement) have brought to light many resting places of the murdered, and the Gisozi memorial in Kigali still fills up by the thousand with newly found remains. Two hundred and sixty thousand now lie there, a mind-numbingly effective reminder of man's depravity that offers to the world its dignified and moving plea 'Never Again.' But there are still many in exile and prison who refuse to say where they disposed of the bodies, making life much harder for those who are bereaved. For those left behind, that lack of information makes the grieving stretch endlessly ahead. Their struggle to forgive is among the hardest, but still there are true examples of the power of Jesus Christ to lift up the broken-hearted to a place of healing and hope.

Others who face the steepest challenge live among their attackers. Most killing was by local *interahamwe* who planned and executed the killing of Tutsis from their local community. Children who survived would suddenly see a man wearing the shirt of their murdered father, women would cower before the shameless gaze of those who had raped them, survivors would walk past the homes of those who had hunted them down, beaten them senseless and left them for dead. There is a Rwandan saying that 'the way to heaven passes by the bed of your enemy'; and this is proven in such cases.

To forgive when justice is done, remorse evident or the pain eased is one thing. To forgive in the face of defiance, mockery and the ever-present reminders of injustice and horror is another. This is the remarkable story of one woman who found the grace to forgive.

Odette Kayitesi lived in a typical mud-brick, cement-plastered Kigali home. There was an old table, a few wobbly chairs and a deep hole in the ground for a toilet, but there was also laughter and joy and hope. Odette was young, pretty and intelligent, and lived in the centre of a community dominated by Hutu neighbours. She had been brought up in a Christian family and taught to love and pray for the poor, the sick and her neighbours. When the genocide began, fear spread like a brushfire, surrounding and trapping villages, neighbourhoods and cities in a helpless panic. Over the radio station RTLM came an incessant message: 'Kill or be killed.' Convinced they would either be killed by Tutsis rising up to defend themselves or by *interahamwe* who would brand them as sympathisers, ordinary men and women turned traitor and became killers. Odette could feel the cold fear of death as the eyes of her neighbours betrayed their intentions. With the roads blocked at every corner and packs of killers roaming the streets, her helpless waiting was quickly confirmed when her neighbours turned her over to the *interahamwe*.

Dragged from her home she was taken to the nearby roadblock, two simple cement road poles doubling as killing posts. The red-brown dust was stained with the blood of those already dispatched and swiftly the machetes came down on the head and neck of Odette until, convinced she was dead, the killers turned for the next helpless victim.

But God was determined she would live. She was thrown onto a truck laden with the bodies of the dead. But the breath of life was still in her body. A looter moved through the bodies on the truck pillaging jewellery and money. As he raked through Odette's pockets a flicker of life betrayed her still-beating heart, and mercilessly the looter thrust a bayonet through her chest. Below her collarbone the scar still bears testimony to God's call in saving her life. The memories are still vivid, and Odette flinches as she recalls that day. Flung into a mass grave, an endless sea of mangled bodies, she clung to life and was found, still breathing, by a Hutu doctor who took her to a hospital. By the time she arrived she was considered dead and placed in the morgue, but a doctor found her there with her heart beating and gave her the kiss of life.

Overwhelmed by the injured and dying, the hospital also had to cope with numerous raids by the militia finishing off survivors. A young woman who was part of Odette's charismatic church group brought food for her each day. The woman's father was a soldier and threatened to kill both of them but the lady simply answered: 'I'd rather die than give up Jesus and what he wants me to do.' Even in the midst of the carnage and pain, Odette found her faith growing in the knowledge that God was looking after her. With her wounds infected by maggots,

Odette was smuggled out of the hospital and rescued by Rwandan Patriotic Front fighters desperately trying to wrest control of the city from the government army.

After the genocide she began to fellowship with other orphans and widows, both at Solace Ministries and at her charismatic group. When Jean Gakwandi of Solace first met Odette he found her constantly weeping, deeply scarred with machete wounds across her face, head and neck, and deeply wounded inside. The pain in her heart and the difficulty of bringing up her younger sister had robbed her of the desire to live, but the prayer support and fellowship in her groups with Hutus began to open her heart to what God was about to do.

One night God gave Odette a vivid dream. 'Jesus was showing me one of my executioners,' she explained, 'but he was very ugly, full of scabies and very thin. Then Jesus told me: "Forgive what he did against you because I forgave too."' She answered the Lord that she would indeed forgive this man, and the anger inside evaporated and was replaced with a new joy and peace. 'Since that time I got to be happy,' is how Odette describes it, and a few days later God gave her another dream, but this time the man was in good health and safe. 'When I remembered how the man was before I forgave him, I understood how forgiveness could save someone and make them a new person too.'

Odette calmly prefaces what happened next with the explanation, 'I knew God was telling me . . .' Obedience to the voice of God came at a high price, but it reaped a rich harvest. Her own home had been razed to the ground by the *interahamwe*. Where her house had stood there was simply the rubble of crumbling mud bricks. At the back of the house the pit latrine was filled up, a sub-terranean tower of bodies covered by hastily thrown-on mud.

As she walked the dusty roads of Kigali, taking shelter in the homes of friends and family, Odette passed those who had dragged her, hit her with a machete and left her for dead. She knew their houses, she walked past their front doors, and she came face to face with them round corners and at the market. But the voice of God called her to forgive, to incarnate the One who incarnated God for us. She walked up to their doors, watched as her attackers opened the door, and offered them forgiveness.

'I also pardoned my neighbours who had given me over to the killers instead of saving me,' she adds. 'I remembered how Jesus behaved when the crowd screamed: "Crucify Him!" As he forgave them all, so do I forgive!'

She went back to the site of her house among her neighbours who had betrayed her, and started to rebuild. When the cost became too high to continue building, Solace was able to provide the money to finish the house. In the corner of the plot of land upon which Odette's new home was built there is a small mound. It covers that deep pit latrine filled with the bodies of those around Odette who didn't survive. But what stands out clear and above contradiction is the power and humility of those who have walked through the valley of the shadow of death and come out with hearts that can still forgive, conquering darkness by the power of the cross. Odette is one of those.

7

Worth More Than That

Personally and nationally, the issue of rape for survivors is on a massive scale in Rwanda. For those women who were not killed outright there were two common outcomes. Either they were kept as sex slaves, often being forcibly married to their captors and given their lives in exchange for sex; or they were raped by *interahamwe*, particularly by known HIV carriers, with the express purpose of either killing them through the brutality of the rape or leaving them to die slowly of HIV/AIDS.

Rape was not an individual man's obscene choice, but a tool of genocide used against the Tutsi women and girls. The purpose was to inflict pain, to humiliate, to infect with HIV, and to kill. No one knows for sure how many women were raped during the genocide, as many rape survivors have never reported it to any authorities for fear of the stigma attached. Those who were raped and killed can of course never speak up, but the UN has made an estimate of between a quarter and half a million. Whatever the numbers, the outcome is that a large proportion of the surviving women are forced to deal not only with the horrific killings of their families, but with their own personal battles against the trauma of brutal rape.

In her book *Proud of Me*[25] Charlene Smith, a survivor
of rape in South Africa and a journalist who has spent
much time investigating and advocating on behalf of
those who have been raped, says: 'Rape is not an event
that happens on a single day. For the survivor it is a
recurrent nightmare for the rest of her life.' The South
African Law Commission has stated that 'rape is not
comparable to any other form of violent crime . . . rape
violates a victim's physical safety, their sexual and psychological integrity. Rape is invasive, dehumanising and
humiliating. It is a crime akin to torture.'[26]

As if that were not bad enough, many rape survivors
in Rwanda suffered added anguish and trauma. These
were multiple rapes, and as the groups of killers usually
numbered more than twenty, the rape could be likewise.
Such rapes were nearly always carried out publicly to
humiliate the woman and frequently the rape of the
woman, and her daughters with her if they were present, occurred in front of their husbands. Sometimes the
preferred method was for the women to be made to
watch their husbands being killed and then raped. Often
they were expressly told that the purpose of their rape
was to kill them – 'we will rape you till you die' was a
threat that was often obscenely fulfilled.

Men with HIV/AIDS were especially prominent in
rape, and if a woman was not raped to death she was
often told by infected men as they raped her that she
would die the slow death of AIDS. Many were raped
before being thrown into rivers to be drowned. Others
had their breasts and sexual organs mutilated, and
unspeakable atrocities were carried out with sharp
implements, sticks, knives, spears, broken bottles and
gun barrels. Women were kept as sex slaves and forcibly
raped by many different men over weeks until they died
or were rescued, and many begged for death before it

came. Hutu women who had married Tutsi men were often also raped as a punishment.

Clementine was one of those who had endured terrible pain and heartache in 1994. She fled to a church for refuge with four thousand others, who were then betrayed by the priest to the *interahamwe* and killed. She was just a seventeen-year-old teenager at the time, and was taken out of the church and raped by a group of fifteen *interahamwe* until she passed out, presumed dead. The militia took a car battery and poured the acid over her genital area, inflicting horrific injuries. Eventually she was hospitalised in Belgium and presented to President Bill Clinton and many others as an example of the suffering the Rwandan people have endured. Unimpressed by all the attention and the spotlights, she returned to her mud-brick home with a small table and a few rickety chairs on the mud floor for furniture. One time, speaking through a nosebleed from AIDS-related illness, she was adamant that what she had found in Christ's love at Solace Ministries far outweighed shaking hands with Presidents and dignitaries. 'At last I have people who listen to me and love me,' she said quietly. Tragically, she was to die soon afterwards, but her last months were lived with some restoration of peace and hope to her life.

Some women were raped over a hundred times. Although conception is rare in rape it does happen, and with a quarter to half a million rapes there are many women who had their own children killed, only to find themselves bearing the children of those who had raped them and killed their families. Surely for those did Christ bear their grief and carry their sorrows, and was scourged for their healing (Is. 53:3-5).

For many who were raped the problem is compounded by stigmatisation by relatives and neighbours.

Ironically some women will only talk to male counsellors because they are afraid the women will gossip and tell their friends and neighbours. They are sometimes despised not only by others, but also by themselves. A deep humiliation came upon those who were raped. The guilt, the contamination, the self-loathing, the fear of men, the shame, all combine to destroy their ability to relate and function normally.

The violence, hatred and humiliation with which those rapes were carried out has created especially deep psychological and emotional wounds, as well as leaving many survivors with major internal injuries and pain. Vestine Kagwera* was brutally multiple-raped and left for dead. Her internal injuries were such that, well over a decade after the injuries were inflicted, each month during her monthly cycle she suffers excruciating pain. The pain triggers the post-traumatic stress originally caused by the rapes and she is unable to afford the medical treatment needed to ease the monthly trauma. It is a terrible legacy to live with, the innocent survivor suffering the constant reminder of her own unjust treatment. When one of the Solace Ministries workers was asked: 'If there was one person whose life you could really change, who would it be?' her reply came back immediately: 'I would like to pay for Vestine to get hospital treatment for her injuries and live without the monthly trauma of her rape.'

Some survivors who were raped castigate themselves for staying alive while others died, refusing rape and choosing death. Uwizera Muzungu Tharcille, the lone survivor of a family of seven, saw her sisters and cousins and many other girls offered their lives if they agreed to go to an *interahamwe's* house for sex. They all refused and were thrown into a pit and stoned to death, including a two-year-old baby girl. It was the third time

Tharcille had been in that situation – the first time, a neighbour's daughter had narrowly escaped when she replied to an *interahamwe* demanding sex, 'I would rather die than sin against God,' and she herself was bought by a neighbour for a drink and told to come home with him and be his wife (she was twelve). When Tharcille refused, he began to beat her with a club, but she managed to escape from the house and walk eleven hours through the night to safety.

The problem of HIV/AIDS is huge. Of those who were raped and survived, an estimated 70-75 per cent were left with HIV/AIDS. Less than a third of Rwandans can afford basic health care, never mind expensive AIDS treatment. A woman left with HIV fears remarriage because of the possibility of infecting her new husband. For younger girls (and some as young as four were raped), even with anti-retroviral drugs, the thought of life without the possibility of marriage is a lonely one.

Another legacy of the genocide is an unequal balance of men and women. Although women and children were killed in huge numbers there was a greater determination to kill men, especially because some women were spared for sexual purposes. In 1998, estimates put the gender ratio in the 25-29 age group as 100:69 women to men.[27] Such an imbalance, and the difficulty of women remarrying if they have internal injuries, has led to a high proportion of widows bringing up their families alone, often with the extra surviving children of relatives. The lack of an adult male makes time spent tending crops difficult, which in turn reduces the possibility of extra crops being sold for cash, increasing the rates of poverty among surviving women and their families. Drug abuse, depression, anxiety and behavioural problems are common, particularly among the younger women and girls.

Men who saw what their wives went through are also deeply traumatised. Many were made to watch them brutally raped by one man after another. The men who somehow survived will often say they would rather have died than see what they were forced to watch, and Emmanuel Mugabo's* comment is typical: 'My wife was raped in front of me by man after man and then killed, but I was spared because I was a Hutu. I'm afraid, ten years later, to get married or to consider any woman as my wife.'

The anti-AIDS message which has been sent out in some African countries, and has led to a marked reduction in infection rates, is now being sent out in Rwanda – A, B, C: Abstain, Be faithful, Condoms, in that order. The government is working hard to source funds for ARV (anti-retroviral) drugs, and there are some figures to suggest the rate of infection is now reducing. But ARV drugs are only effective when diet and general health are good, and the poverty and food shortages which many widows experience also have to be combated if recovery is to be assured.

Although there is some practical response in terms of health care, and although HIV and rape survival organisations are seeking justice for victims, the emotional wounds of the genocide cannot be treated by drugs or healed by courts of law. All over Rwanda there are women who were confined to their beds awaiting death, who have made great progress with ARV drugs. But for many, the wounds in their hearts are still very fresh. A study five years after the genocide suggested that over 80 per cent of survivors were still traumatised by their ordeal, and time itself does not heal such deep trauma.[28] For many Rwandans there is simply nowhere to go to talk through their anguish, and there seems only one solution – to numb the pain and live as though emotionally dead, internalising their trauma. The result is that their mental health is jeopardised and they are at risk of suicide.

The challenge to bring healing to the traumatised rape survivors of Rwanda is very great, but God's people are rising to that challenge. This is the story of Diane,* her struggle to stay alive until she wished for death itself, and her brave response to the love of God.

Brought up as one of nine children, Diane was twenty years old when the genocide began. She lived in the east of Rwanda in a rural sector of the district of Bicumbi, called Rubona. When the killing began she had fled with a group of children to a neighbouring sector, into a plantation of sorghum, a crop like millet that grows to about six feet, with long green stalks and reddy-brown heads of grain about eight inches high. Her mother, father and eight brothers and sisters never made it that far. They were beaten and hacked to death, along with thirty thousand other helpless victims in that area of ten square miles.

For five days Diane hid among the sorghum, listening to the endless screams and cries of the victims. Once she was discovered and severely beaten, but her attackers failed to kill her. After five days she crept out of the sorghum and risked returning to her home. It was an awful sight with mutilated bodies littering the ground; her house was no longer there, having been reduced to a pile of mud rubble. Diane had no choice but to hunt among the corpses until she found her family's bodies among the scattered, twisted victims.

The killing continued and those who survived the first days were hunted down, beaten and cut to death. With no home, Diane went back to the fields and hid. She found two women who had survived, but the area was overrun with *interahamwe* who systematically scoured the fields for survivors and soon the three of them were discovered. The two women were killed, one being thrown into a latrine where many bodies had been dumped. Diane remembers she was still alive when they threw her down. Many who survived the genocide and even those who took part are troubled most by those images of bleeding victims flailing desperately as mud was piled over their broken but still living bodies.

Unable to escape detection Diane was also caught and her captors began to beat her, especially around the head. They rained down blows on her body, breaking her leg. She was not far from death, but suddenly she heard the chief of the group call a halt. They had decided to spare her life: at twenty years old she could make the *interahamwe* a captive wife. In mocking humiliation the chief decreed: 'Let's not kill her, but we'll marry her to the ugliest of all of us.' As Diane lay broken and wounded they argued among themselves what fate should befall her. Finally she was put up for sale, to be auctioned to the highest bidder.

The bids are still clear in her memory: they started at 2,000 Rwandese francs (about £2.50), then 5,000 francs. It was not enough for the chief, who wanted to make some money out of the sale, and they were turned down. Diane knew what awaited her as a sex slave 'wife', and begged them to kill her instead and end the horror and pain. She remembers one man saying: 'I want to tear her and eat her heart.' In the demonic terror of the genocide she knew it was no idle threat. There are cases in that province of genocide victims having their hearts and livers torn out, made into brochettes and roasted and eaten. Another of the group berated those who offered such a 'low price', and cajoled them to kill her and be finished with it. 'If you don't want her, let's get on with it and kill her!' he shouted.

But Diane's life was saved by a bid of 2,000 francs more, and she was bought for 7,000 francs (about £10 then). The winner's prize was to rape her in front of the crowd. Diane longed for death to overtake her.

Brought up a charismatic Catholic, her faith in God was shattered, and the possibility that God could exist disappeared in the nightmare she was living. She was taken home by the *interahamwe* who had bought her. Still longing for death she seized an opportunity to hang herself on a tree with a simple cord, but a Hutu girl saw her and accused her of committing a sin by killing herself: 'You should go to the killers and ask them to kill you instead.'

Every day the *interahamwe* would check she was still held in captivity but as time went by they started to regret she was still alive, because few Tutsis were left in the area and many killers were dedicated to complete extermination. But her captor was not going to give up his prize, and she was hidden and escaped death again.

Eventually the RPF overran Bicumbi and Diane was rescued, pregnant with the child of her captor. Despite the manner of its conception, Diane had no one else in the world left, and hoped for some solace in the birth of her child. 'I wanted to see a child from my sorrows and pains,' she explains. But even that wish was denied her, as the child was stillborn.

She was left disabled, with no home and no strength or ability to plough her field and produce some food. 'I had fear and sorrow, and kept to myself, she says. A gastric ulcer didn't help, and night-time brought insomnia and nightmares. Though she wanted to cry continually there was no one to cry with and she bore her grief alone, her pain boiling into anger and bitterness. 'I hated everyone,' she remembers, 'and I hated God.'

It is 2002 and Diane, now 28, is still in shock. One of the leaders of a Solace group, a woman called Leocadia, is in the area, and she begins to comfort Diane and brings her into the safety of God's people at Solace. Like many who had hidden themselves away in their sorrow and given up hope of healing, Diane is 'astonished' to find people who care for her and love her. Her whole inner being was destroyed, but the love of Jesus Christ was able to restore it. It is true that 'love never fails' (1 Cor. 13:8), and above all else those who have been so horrifically raped and abused need the genuine, unconditional love of God for their healing. When that love is shown through people whose lives are laid down in sacrificial help for them, Christ's command to love and serve is seen in the restoration of broken hearts, bodies and souls.

Uwimana Denise counsels and prays with many of the rape survivors who come to Solace. 'Those who have been raped are often more deeply wounded and traumatised than those who were not,' she says. Although all the survivors have deep wounds and trauma because of what they have seen and experienced, including the death of their loved ones, those who were raped suffered one of the ugliest atrocities in the genocide. The effects of rape, apart from the high incidence of HIV infection, include injuries to the vertebrae, complete loss of functioning female organs, persistent infections and severe headaches. 'Many of them they have no desire to live at all,' Denise explains. 'They have completely lost any trust in anyone, their faith in God is destroyed because they believe God rejected them and did not protect them. They live with a sense of shame and many are afraid to mix with others, always afraid that people might know what has happened to them. Those who have tears are constantly crying, for others there is just a numb, dry, deadness in their eyes.'

Denise is repeatedly faced with women who live in what she calls 'lamentations and loneliness', who have no idea where hope can come from and least of all expect it from God. Of crucial importance is the break in the link between the rapist and the survivor. 'You cannot break the link between the rapist and the survivor without the strength from the blood of Jesus,' she says. 'The rapists tortured them in a way that was demonic and not human.'

Denise has had to minister to a girl who is receiving help at Solace after she was raped at the age of four and infected with HIV/AIDS. As well as personal counselling and prayer, Denise encourages women rape survivors to come to the fellowship meetings. There a combination of worship and praise, preaching and testimony helps the women to share their experiences, discover they are not alone in their trauma, open up to the healing of the cross and begin to trust again.

The fellowship meetings and individual counselling and ministry sessions continue together, as well as a programme of visitation by Solace workers or volunteers from the fellowship groups that have formed. The women's health is checked and they are encouraged to go for HIV tests. Denise is clear in her focus, of encouraging survivors

- to see God in the church and not in people, who are imperfect
- to realise God made them survivors for a purpose
- to not be ashamed of what has happened
- to understand God loves them
- to understand God has a plan for their lives
- to become an example to others.

She describes a recent camp where orphans who were raped were being comforted and encouraged: 'I told them that God loves them and has a good plan for their

lives. I told them that if they walk humbly and obey
God, God as their Father will restore them, will comfort
them and their future will shine with joy. God will give
them a new family. I asked them to be a good example.'

After being comforted, the recovering women often
choose to go back to their churches for fellowship and help.
I ask Denise whether many consider marrying or remarrying. 'For the widows, our culture does not make it easy to
remarry. But we know that God allows them to remarry
and I have talked to some who have said that if they can get
somebody who cares, who listens to them, and who under-
stands the situation, they are willing to remarry. For the
younger girls, because they lost parents and relatives, they
need someone who can be both husband and parents.'

There are constant challenges in the ministry to rape
survivors: for the survivors themselves, difficulties of
travel for those who live in rural areas far from a decent
road, and problems of accommodation for those staying
with relatives but having to leave; for their carers, the
need to provide good food to help the ARV drugs for
HIV/AIDS become effective, and the organisation of fellowship groups providing support, training and work
experience to generate an income.

The Solace workers follow the lead of their director,
Jean Gakwandi, who is careful not to force the forgiveness issue prematurely. They are also careful to separate
forgiveness from reconciliation – the latter needs trust
which is not possible without repentance from the perpetrator and even then it is not always wise, especially
in cases of rape. But with salvation comes new power
and grace. The anger, hatred and unforgiveness are
released through the cross in God's time, and this brings
further freedom and healing.

For those who knew Diane before she was healed it is
hard to recognise her. She looks so well, so vibrant, so

healthy, so good, and they can only remember the shadow of the broken woman they knew. The faith that the enemy robbed her of is returning as she sees God to be the solution and not the reason for her pain. As God's peace is restored through prayer, love and counselling, Diane sleeps at peace for the first time. Once the healing comes, although memories are not always completely eradicated, their power is broken, and the restoration of the heart is usually followed by transformation of the mind and the whole life. Diane is not shaken when other women begin to talk of their own rapes, and she listens and counsels them effectively.

There is a latent potential and energy in many survivors. When God heals wounds, there can be a beautiful burst of fruitfulness in their lives that often leads to skilled, compassionate and effective help for other survivors. Diane has taken on responsibility for a group of widows and orphans at Bicumbi, where a high proportion of Tutsis were killed and an estimated thirty thousand of the sixty thousand population were slaughtered. With her ordeal now behind her, she has a hope and a future and is determined to share it with as many people as she can.

8

The Pain of Loss

It is several years after the genocide, and a group of widows is singing. The bright yellows, greens and reds of their ethnic printed dresses fill the room with colour as their voices rise and fall with the African beat. They clap the rhythm out and some of them sway to the tempo, but others are still clearly struggling to worship with any sense of joy, and their bereavement and loss are palpable. They sing a common song among the widows that speaks of God's grace in sparing their lives:

Niki wayihaye iyo Mana yawe?
What have you given to your God?
Mbese n'iki wayihaye iyo Mana yawe?
What have you given to your God?

Abasore barapfuye urasigara
Young men died and you remained.
Mbese n'iki wayihaye iyo Mana yawe?
What have you given to your God?

Ntacyo nayihaye iyo Mana yanjye
Nothing have I given to my God.

Ni ubuntu yangiriye iyo Mana yanjye
It is only by the grace of my God.

Abandi barapfuye urasigara
Others died and you remained.

For many widows, the very act of being thankful to be alive is a new experience, and a significant stepping stone on the road to healing and recovery. Those who saw loved ones killed and lost all their family and relatives often identify with those who died more strongly than with those who remain. Year after year goes by and they still yearn to be with the dead rather than the living, and many have taken their own lives.

The Bible speaks frequently of God as the Restorer – of health, of freedom, of worship, of souls, of joy, of comfort and of life. The chorus of Psalm 80, 'O God, restore us, And cause Your face to shine upon us and we will be saved' (v. 3; see also vs 7,19), combines the desire for recovery from disaster, a new experience of the presence of God and his favour, and the saving intervention of God. It reflects the need of the widows and, when they are too broken to utter it themselves, it is the prayer of those who have been healed for those who still suffer.

Beata Mukarubuga was one of those for whom a prolonged life after the genocide seemed even worse than death. The deep loneliness she felt combined with the horror and pain of her loved ones' deaths to drive her ever deeper into depression.

Mama Lambert, as she is affectionately known, grew up in the rolling hills of Nyanza in the south of Rwanda. Her life was reasonably comfortable because her father owned a good number of cattle, as well as working in a dairy nearby. She sums up her life before 1994 with the simple words: 'We had milk to drink.' Twenty-four hours after President Habyarimana's plane was shot down on the evening of 6 April, clouds of smoke were already rising ominously from the nearby province of Gikongoro and her life was about to change forever. During the first few days of the genocide, there was a short lull before the storm as her district of Nyanza was spared the ferocious early onslaught of the killing. Tutsi refugees began to arrive from surrounding areas, some of them still herding their precious cattle before them, and they slept out on a hill near Beata's house called Mount Gacu.

The situation turned much worse with the arrival of the *Gendarmerie* (the military police), and Beata remembers the sound of gunfire all through the night as the refugees on the hill were gunned down. Those that escaped fled to the swamps and forests, but the organisation of genocide was turning its attention ever more strongly to Nyanza. Although many of the ordinary Hutus at Nyanza had refused to start killing, RTLM, the radio station pumping out hatred and instructions for the genocide, marked out Beata's district to be attacked as soon as possible. The burgomasters of the area were summoned to a meeting on 18 April and two days later the Presidential Guard arrived in the area. The next day roadblocks were set up and groups of killers began to patrol the area.

Tuzabatsembatsemba ('We will exterminate them') they chanted over and over again, as they started the day with a huge slaughter of the Tutsis' cattle. Beata's husband went for help to the local officials, but was told the only help he would get was to be killed with a gun instead of a machete, as the official decree of the government was that all Tutsis must die. As he arrived back at the house with his grim news, a Tutsi neighbour married to a Hutu begged them to flee, telling them breathlessly: 'People are being killed everywhere and your names are on the list to be killed. They are coming to take the petrol from your husband's motorbike to burn the house down.'

It was a warning that left little time, and their indecision had fatal consequences: within five minutes her husband was bundled into a truck packed with Tutsis and driven off. Beata was never to see him again, alive or dead. With eight children to look after and to shelter from the growing spread of killing, she sent three to hide at the house of the woman who had warned them minutes before, one fled with the house girl, two others she sent to an elderly Tutsi man they believed might be spared, one went to his godfather and the youngest, not yet a toddler, she put on her back and fled to the marshes, then to the bushes, and finally to the sorghum plantations.

The next weeks were a constant turmoil of hiding and fleeing. The killers searched the bushes and fields, often with dogs to track down survivors. As she fled from one such hunt she arrived at the home of a godly man called Isaka. He hid her for several days, but news came to him that the killers were coming for her the next morning, and during the night he told her to flee and put a Bible in her hand. 'Do you think those who died did not have Bibles?' Mama Lambert asked incredulously. 'Is this Bible a gun or a grenade, or at least a machete I can fight my aggressors with?' Isaka looked at her calmly: 'God has shown me you will survive,' he spoke prophetically. 'I also will live and we shall meet, and you will tell me how you survived.'

Day after day Mama Lambert and her son cheated death, fell into rivers and hid in marshes and bushes as mobs of killers hunted the area and shouted slogans. Some of her neighbours who were part of the local *interahamwe* knew she had survived and saw her walking up

a hill. Mama Lambert heard their shouts and ran for her
life, with the mob running in a deadly chase up the hill
behind her. She ran into a place where some local Twa
had a pottery compound, and hid among the pots (the
Twa are a pygmy tribe that live as a small minority in
Rwanda and are skilled in pottery making). The woman
there felt sorry for her and feigned hatred for any Tutsis
when the mob charged in – 'We have nothing in common with the Tutsis,' she answered them. 'I wish she
was here and then when she is taken to be killed I can
have her clothes.'

Mama Lambert's heart pounded so loudly she was
convinced she was hearing the footsteps of the killers
among the pots, but the woman's bluster won out and
the killers left. She made some sorghum porridge for
Mama Lambert and the baby, but her son was involved
in the genocide and shortly afterwards arrived home,
carrying loot from the homes of murdered Tutsis.
Furious that his mother had spared a Tutsi, he took his
sword and made to kill her. With the sword at Mama
Lambert's chest ready to strike, the Twa woman pleaded
for her life. The son relented and threw Mama Lambert
and her son out of the compound, but another group of
killers was roaming the area and she was immediately
seen and captured. The killers were herding Tutsis
together, and when about eighty had been gathered they
took them to the edge of a mass grave and put them in
lines of male and female. Then they took their machetes
and began to strike and kill, throwing the dead and
dying into the grave.

The memories of that time are very strong for Mama
Lambert. She remembers the sound of people praying
and singing, the words of the song *Glory to God* suddenly being cut off as voices disappeared, the *Ave Maria*
mingling with the desperate cries of children. 'I promise

not to wet my bed,' one child cried, and others pleaded for mercy, promising they would not be Tutsis any more. The killers laughed as some children shouted: 'We will tell our dads if you kill us.'

As the line was chopped down Mama Lambert waited, transfixed in fear, until a man who had been a fellow pupil pulled her out of the queue just four people before her turn to be killed. 'I don't want to see you being killed,' he said as he sent her off to hide in the bushes. 'You can die another day.' Mama Lambert hid in the bushes of Gatagara, near a centre for handicapped people, who were mercilessly hunted down with dogs and killed. A dog also found her but she took the Bible Isaka had given her and threw it at the dog, which turned and left. The smell of rotting bodies became ever more overpowering, and her baby boy Lambert grew silent from hunger and thirst. Believing she was watching him die, she cried out desperately to God: 'If this child doesn't die, I will praise you.'

It was a promise she would take several years to fulfil.

Weary of carrying her heavy Bible, she threw it away. As her eyes followed its flight she saw the bramble bushes heavily laden with fruit, where it landed. Hurriedly she squashed the berries and offered their juice to Lambert. He began to revive, and for the next eleven days she fed him on crushed fruit juice. 'I thank God for that day when he gave us manna,' she says.

Later she decided to venture to the home of a man to whom her husband had given a cow some years earlier. His response was to chase her away and tell her the terrible news that no Tutsis were alive, including her own children. The news was too much for Mama Lambert – her children murdered, only her baby left – and she

walked on to the dusty road, deranged with grief, crying and shouting: 'Oh my children! Oh my children!'
Not caring any more about her own life she arrived at a
roadblock, still crying and shouting. Women in the fields
nearby began to pelt her with stones, and a man at the
roadblock gave her a beating and told her to go and get
killed elsewhere. She walked right into the house of one
of the killers' ringleaders. His eyes met hers with surprise as he exclaimed: 'How are you still alive?' He
checked his register and, confused, said: 'You are down
here as dead.'

　'My husband and children have been killed – please
kill me with a gun and not a machete,' she implored
him. By now the RPF troops were not far away and making rapid progress against the government forces. The
man's wife, Mukasine,* argued with him: 'Spare her life
and the RPF might spare us.' She gave Lambert some
milk and helped Beata to hide in the house as soldiers
swarmed around the area, the sound of mortars and
gunfire growing louder each day. Suddenly the boom of
mortars and rat-tat-tat of gunfire went silent and soldiers, killers and residents fled from the approaching
RPF. The only sound was the bleating of goats and the
crying of lost children.

　Mama Lambert emerged out into the sunshine to find
the RPF outside. 'Why did you arrive too late to save my
husband and children?' she cried in anguish. She would
soon discover that more than her husband and children
had been killed. Her 68-year-old mother had been forced
to watch thirty-four of her children and grandchildren
killed before her eyes. 'We want you to die of sorrow,'
the killers taunted, but she offered them money to kill
her too and spare her any more anguish. She was taken
up on her offer and they walked her eight miles before
throwing her into a river with one of her cousins and

four of her children. The children drowned but the cousin was a strong swimmer and managed to swim to the shore with Beata's mother. When it was discovered she had survived, the *interahamwe* paid a man two hundred Rwandan francs (25 pence) to go and kill her and throw her body into a pit latrine.

Mama Lambert's father's fate was no better. When the killing began, he went to the burgomaster to ask for help but was immediately grabbed and put into a lorry and taken to the river. There, because he was a particularly tall Tutsi, and because he had many cows and worked in a dairy, the killers told him they would cut him in pieces to shorten him and see if his blood was made of milk. At eighty-two years old he was cut to pieces with machetes and the pieces thrown into the river.

With her house destroyed, her family killed and her neighbours responsible for most of that destruction, Beata stayed a few miles away at Ruhango. Too distraught to sleep at night and too shattered to think during the day, her days and nights merged into one long search for relief. A deep emptiness filled her heart and her mind numbed itself into oblivion. There were no friends or family left, just herself and baby Lambert, and she wept continuously. The horror of what she had seen raised a further complication – she was one of the few witnesses left to many of the killings. It was not a rare thing for witnesses to be killed to stop them testifying about the involvement of members of their communities, and she moved to the capital Kigali for safety.

Life continued to spiral downwards, and she decided to throw herself into the River Nyabarongo and join those who had died in its waters. The day she and another woman were on their way to drown themselves, a cousin of her husband who had survived met her and said: 'I know a man who can help and comfort you.' The

cousin, Droscella, had met Jean Gakwandi and found
Solace Ministries to be a place of hope and healing.
Mama Lambert agreed to the offer, and found herself
walking into Solace and breaking down in tears with the
other widows. It was a window of hope, and as she
began to return regularly and took the opportunity to
share her pain, the frozen numbness began to thaw. 'I
felt some comfort and I started to become a human
being,' she recalls. 'I started to sleep for the first time in
two years and to get friends and a new family. I received
Jesus into my heart and he became my Lord. He became
my refuge and he took off all my burdens.'

She had another surprise awaiting her, as two of her
other children had survived and tracked her down after
two years. One son, Dieudonne, had seen his sisters, a
grandmother and an aunt being killed and had been
afflicted with speech difficulties; and Denise, one of
Mama Lambert's daughters, was taken by the housegirl
to the Congo and saw many horrific sights of suffering
and death. Mama Lambert also took in six orphans to
her home to care for them, and says: 'I thank God who
helped the children I care for; they are all in secondary
school and two are at university. Jesus comes to help me
in all our troubles.'

Mama Lambert has been strengthened in her faith,
and is an inspiration to hundreds of the widows who
come to Solace for help. The reality of her transformation from hopelessness to hope is always present. 'My
faith was shattered,' she states, 'but after I received salvation and read the word of God I saw how Jesus and
Job, Naomi, Ruth, Joseph, Stephen and others went
through difficulties and I was strengthened. I was weary
and he gave me rest. He came to my help and gave me
salvation and hope. Jesus is on the throne of my heart
and he strengthens me.'

Although God was healing her heart, she still faced the struggle of dealing with the aftermath of the genocide. 'I hated everybody after the genocide,' she confesses. 'I even hated Mukasine, who saved me from the hands of her husband, because I could only think of her husband and not see any goodness in her.'

In 2000 Beata received two letters from Ephraim Balinda.* In them he told her how he had killed people including her family, and asked forgiveness. Ephraim lives with constant nightmares about those he killed, and he pleaded not just with Beata but with God, the President, all Rwanda and the whole world to forgive him. He detailed where the bodies were dumped, and Beata and other survivors found 127, including her children, her mother-in-law, her sister-in-law and her baby. She breaks out in prayer: 'I thank everyone, O my God, everyone who gave back dignity to my children the day they were taken out of pit latrines and were buried now as human beings.'

She continues to say: 'I thank everyone who intervened for the memorial built for them. This was something that touched my heart after 1994.' The memorial for the 127 victims from that pit is a simple, neat brick wall with a white plaque and a white cross silhouetted against the green trees and hills behind it. There is part of Isaiah 26:19 inscribed on the plaque: 'Your dead will live, their corpses will rise.' Along the top of the plaque are the words *urwibutso rw'inzirakarengane zazize itsembabwoko ryo mu 1994* – 'Remember the innocent victims: refuse the senseless killing of 1994'. There lie five of her children. Her husband has never been found and those who know where his body was thrown refuse to tell.

Dealing with Ephraim's letters was a difficult process for Beata. 'I had to keep praying about it because I felt he should be killed as well,' she says honestly. After she spent months praying God gave her the grace to forgive: 'Forgiveness is a process that is based on what Jesus did on the cross. I could not bear even to see his face but now I can greet him [he has been released from prison] because I forgave him.'

After the struggle to forgive Ephraim was resolved, she began to visit others in prison. Mukasine, the wife of the man she describes as 'a terrible *genocidaire*', was also in prison and she began to visit her, prayed with her and led her to give her life to the Lord. There are many others who took part in the killing in her area who are also in the jail, and she encourages them to turn to God and repent and ask for forgiveness. They find such grace in Beata hard to understand and still struggle with their own guilt, though her testimony and kindness have deeply touched some of them. The testimony of how God kept her alive to use her for his glory gives hope to those who struggle under the burdens of their experiences.

Most especially, her testimony of how God healed the terrible emptiness of the loss of friends and family encourages them to believe that their pain may be healed also. Beata travels throughout Rwanda encouraging, ministering and organising. Her home area of Nyanza has received new cattle from Solace, and she beamed with happiness when the survivors of Nyanza sang and danced as they named each cow. She works especially hard in the counselling of unhealed widows and orphans. 'They have very great trauma and some of them come to us saying they would rather be dead than alive. The most affecting issue is the wound inside, and so we set up days to visit them and counsel them. Sometimes they don't like to share and want to keep it to themselves, but then they become secure and trust us and become open to share and be healed.'

Beata is now part of the leadership team of Solace, helping organise and carry through its ministry to forty-two groups across Rwanda, each with one or two hundred widows and orphans. I watch her as she comforts one of the orphans. She has the bearing of a kindly matron, serious but gentle, her dark black hair braided and tied back, her eyes concentrating firmly, and her words full of wisdom. She has received a gift from God to comfort others, and she serves them with grace, authority and compassion. She has only three of her eight children to pour out her love on, but there are many hundreds of others who have received her comfort with grateful hearts.

9

Innocence Lost

This is the story of Uwineza and other children. More than a decade after the genocide, Uwineza* recalls her ninth year with a terrible vividness.

I was born in 1985, the youngest of nine children, five boys and four girls. My mother's name was Esperance and my father was Nzaramba.* We were brought up as Roman Catholic Christians, and our father used to call us together to pray and read the Bible. We were neighbours to an orphanage, and dad used to tell us that God loves orphans and that we should pray for them. I thought if ever I become an adult I will care for orphans.

Even before the genocide began, we were repeatedly threatened with death and often slept at my dad's office for safety. By the time of the genocide, my parents were separated, and though I normally stayed with my mother, I was with my father. When the killing began, we thought it would only last for a few days and then be over, so we hid at my dad's office, but as the days passed with no food we decided to risk coming out rather than die from hunger.

As soon as we got back home, two soldiers appeared and took my father and an elder brother and started to march them away, beating them violently as they went. They took them to my father's office where he had worked as a tribunal for the province of Butare. By the time they got there they were too beaten to walk, and they were shot and killed. We children ran back home, crying with grief. As soon as we got there, a car full of Presidential Guards came and started shooting and breaking into the house. A brother, a sister and myself ran out the back door and hid in a bush. When the shooting finished we went back home and found everyone dead. My sisters were naked and had been raped: we found a bed sheet and covered them.

We went to a neighbour's house to hide with some others who had escaped but soon afterwards we were found. Although my sister had managed to cover me with grass to hide me, she and my brother were discovered and hacked by machetes. My brother was struck on his neck, and when he fell down they continued on his body and then they cut off his 'sex.' My sister, who was thirteen, was taken by one of those killers and raped; after he had raped her he abandoned her for other killers. She managed to find me again and we hid and ate raw sorghum and sweet potatoes from the ground.

After some days we decided to hide in the house of some people who had been killed, thinking that the killers might not visit that house again. We found a house with some others who were hiding but after a few days we were all discovered by some *interahamwe*. They ordered us to collect dry grass and then they put us in the grass and poured petrol over us. Just as they were about to burn us, my sister and I were recognised by a man who had lost a case my father had presided over and he said he wanted to kill us personally. He made us stand beside him as he burnt the others and we watched them screaming in agony as they were burnt alive. I will never forget this horrible scene – my aunt was among them and she was crying out to us to finish her off and spare her more pain but we could not help.

When they had finished killing and burning, the man took us to his home and made us clean the machete and sword he had been using to kill people that day. We were held captive and in the morning he went and got Solange our cousin, who was also being kept. He told us he would show us something good and raped her before pushing a stick up between her legs, and she died after suffering great pain. He then forced us to carry the body to the pit latrine and throw it down the hole.

The next day he said he was fed up with seeing us and that he had raped enough Tutsis so we should go and be killed by some other killers. When we left, we went to a house to hide and found a woman with the bodies of her dead children. She told us the killers kept her there and came to rape her, and we should run away before they came and did to us what they had done to her children. On the way from that house we met the wife of one of the *interahamwe*, who agreed to hide us as she said no one would suspect there were survivors in her house. It was very hard to stay in the house hidden from her husband and we used to have to hide under the bed while he was in the room. Once we heard him say angrily to his wife that, although they had done a good job, there were still some people who were not accounted for and that 'Nzaramba's daughters' (that was us) were among them. The next day the woman told us it was too dangerous to hide any longer in the house, and she showed us a hole outside where we could hide.

One evening when she was bringing us some food she brought a man who was a friend of my brothers who said he would help us join an orphanage. But he took us to a house and locked the door before returning with one of those who had killed my brother. One of them took my sister into the next room and the other told me to remove my clothes. When I refused, he took a knife and tore the clothes off with his knife. I fought him but I was only nine and he was stronger than me and raped me. There was a lot of blood and I had never felt such pain in my life. When my sister returned, she had been raped as well but she gave me water to drink and washed me. When they came back in the evening, she begged them to leave me because I was so weak and offered herself to be raped by both of them. But they refused and repeated what they had done. It was so sore I shouted and screamed, but he put a cloth in my mouth to stop me shouting and carried on.

My body was racked with pain and in the morning I asked my sister to find a way to kill me. I hated myself and I hated being alive and wanted to die. But my sister persuaded me to stay calm and wait on God alone as he would decide whether we would live or die. When the men came back, my sister begged them to kill us and spare us more pain but instead they wanted us to live in misery and took us to an orphanage. The first orphanage refused us because they said they would not take Tutsis but the second was run by the Red Cross and they took us in. But we were still not safe: even the Red Cross could not keep us safe, because the *interahamwe* used to come into the orphanage and take away the men and boys to kill them, leaving the women and girls to use for themselves. Some mothers started to dress their sons in girls' clothing and a few escaped, but later on the killers removed the children's clothes and killed the boys. Before they killed people, they would offer them a bullet and if they could pay enough money they were shot: if not, they were hacked to death.[29] Then they forced us (the mothers and wives and sisters) to dig the graves and bury the bodies.

When the war started to look bad for the government and the *interahamwe* they decided to escape with us in a lorry container over the border with Burundi. We heard that fifty other children had been taken all the way to Congo before being killed. We were discovered in Burundi and the Burundi government let us go free but three of the children had already died in the container. The Burundi government asked people to adopt us and a Rwandan family took me back to Rwanda after the genocide finished. We found out later a brother had survived but apart from him and my sister, the other six and my parents and relatives were all dead.

I was still in primary school education and I was taken to hospital because of the injuries I had sustained during the rape, but my back has never healed. I was constantly agitated and suffered continual nightmares; I could never smile, I never wanted to talk and I believed that nothing could ever make me happy again. The foster family that kept me were not Christians and never prayed but I never had any desire to seek God either. I believed that the God of before the genocide was not the same as that after the genocide. The only way I could express myself was with tears but I could never talk about why I cried and I had no one to comfort me. I remembered the way my father used to comfort the orphans near our home but I could not find anyone to do for me what he had done for them.

For a nine-year-old girl, it is hard to fathom the damage such an ordeal can do. Is there any way back when the innocence of a young girl is lost like that? Research can show us that rape, the witness of violent killings, sudden and unexpected bereavement and personal injury are frequent triggers to what is known as post-traumatic stress disorder. It can tell us that a child's 'cognitive, social, emotional and physical functioning may all be impacted by trauma, generating a negative outcome for the child's development and mental health.'[30] What it cannot do is take us inside the head and heart of a little girl and let us feel and see her pain, her loneliness and her nightmares.

When Uwineza started secondary school, the pain in her back grew worse and she was constantly sick. At school, she met another orphan whose complete family had been wiped out. She was a born-again Christian and began to pray for Uwineza. Although Uwineza spent much of her time in tears and failed to respond, she continued to be loved by her friend. 'My friend never got discouraged,' she says thankfully. 'She was aware of my situation and knew that I was under the torture of the devil.'

One night, Uwineza had a dream. She had previously made a decision never to mix with any Hutus, but in the dream she found herself surrounded by *interahamwe* in a ghastly scene that assaulted her eyes and ears with horrible sights and smells. She woke up full of fear, and shared it with her friend. The friend and another girl began to pray with Uwineza. 'They told me to pray intensively because the place I saw in the dream was an indication of my spiritual state.'

For Uwineza it was a major effort to start to pray at all. At that point she still would have preferred death rather than life with the trauma. But as she began to pray, little by little she also found strength to start talking about her pain. It was a difficult time to begin any process of healing: the woman in the foster family developed an animosity against her, constantly found fault, tried to marry her off and even stopped giving her any food. When Uwineza decided she could no longer go back to that home, the headmaster of the school looked after her until the family that was looking after her

sister took her in as well. It was a constant struggle to
find food, clothes and money for school, and the continued prayers of her Christian friends had not yet been
answered. But when they invited Uwineza to go with
them to church she encountered God's word in a powerful way

> The preaching was talking about me. I heard many
> voices in my ears saying, God loves you, God loves you.
> I eventually knelt down and bowed without realising
> what I was doing. They prayed for me and I confessed
> and accepted Jesus into my life. I knew that Jesus gave
> his life for me. On 19 February 2002, I got a joy I had
> never known before and that I will never forget; it's a joy
> that even my parents could never give me. I became a
> new being and came to know that God loves orphans.

For Uwineza there were three sources of help that began
to restore her lost innocence and broken heart. The interest that her Christian friends showed, both those from
her church and also those in Solace Ministries where she
began to visit, had a deep effect upon her. As with many
who were traumatised and left alone she suffered from a
combination of depression, anxiety, self-loathing and
loneliness. The importance of quality Christian love and
friendship should never be underestimated in God's
plan of healing. In Psalm 16:3, David exclaims: 'As for
the saints who are in the land, they are the glorious ones
in whom is all my delight.' The loss of her innocence had
left Uwineza with a deep hatred of herself, but the value
those Christian friends put on her began to convince her
she mattered. In addition, she bears witness to the help
Jean Gakwandi of Solace has given her: 'God has given
me a new father in him, and he has integrated me
among his children.' She is still not rid of a last portion

of her insecurity and adds: 'I wonder if I am worth it!' But the love she is experiencing is a demonstration of how precious her life is in the sight of God and his servants.

The second source of support came from her surviving brother and sister. After years apart in various foster families, they joined together to be a family again, albeit a remnant of what once was. Her brother and sister 'are not saved yet', but she testifies that 'God cares for us in a tremendous way and miraculously we have food and clothes.'

It is this knowledge and experience of God's presence that provides the third stream of love for Uwineza. The reality of his presence is what she needed to fill the emptiness and restore her innocence. However much the facts of the attack are evidence that they were not to blame, child victims of rape often struggle with feelings of guilt and shame. The acceptance God provides, and the cleansing of the cross, overturned this burden in Uwineza's heart. It is not just sin that the blood of Jesus covers and washes away, but a condemning conscience. 1 John 3:16-20 explains: 'This is how we know what love is: Jesus Christ laid down his life for us. And we ought to lay down our lives for our brothers . . . this then is how we know we belong to the truth, and how we set our hearts at rest in His presence whenever our hearts condemn us. For God is greater than our hearts, and he knows everything.'

Living in the reality of the love of God and in loving relationships breaks the power of a self-hating conscience and sets us free to enjoy being the children of God. Eugene Peterson's translation of the verses above in *The Message* is particularly adept at pinpointing this: 'Let's practise real love . . . this is the only way we'll know we're living truly, living in God's reality. It's also the way to shut down debilitating self-criticism . . . for God is greater than our worried hearts . . . and once that's taken care of and we're no longer accusing or condemning ourselves, we're bold and free before God!'

It was good for Uwineza to feel clean and whole after years of self-hatred. 'I used to feel really diminished and unworthy, but now I have been comforted I feel like other young girls and I realise I have a new beginning in life.'

The restoration of her life still has some ground to cover. 'I meet a lot of challenges,' she admits, 'but I have One who fights for me and I have a joy that is unshakeable.' But perhaps the most wonderful thing to happen is when love returns to a broken heart. There is nothing that fills an empty heart more fully than love, nothing that restores lost innocence better than love. 'I felt that love was coming into my heart little by little,' she marvels. 'I started to love people and realised how wonderful it was to be in God. God is both Father and Mother to me. I know he never changes and he loves me.'

God continues to give good things to her. 'When God gives to you, he really gives,' she says joyfully. 'He gave me the talent to sing for him and I want to sing for him until he comes back.' She will have to start singing at work now, as her latest good news is that she has just gained some employment! 'I thank him for all that he does for me,' she concludes.

10

Trauma and Nightmares

The whole of Rwanda was immersed in the sudden cataclysm of killing. (In some southern areas, because of tensions between northern and southern Hutus who were vying for power, the killing was delayed by several days, but it soon broke out with its own viciousness.) Those who survived did so through incredible acts of bravery on the part of those who hid them, endangering their own lives. Others survived by the power of God confusing the killers, and by miracles of deliverance. Some survived by hiding in swamps and coming out at night to eat raw roots. Many girls and women survived because they were kept as sex slaves until they were rescued. And some survived because the killers thought they were dead. Of all those who survived, many in this last group have been through the deepest horror of living among the dead.

In many of the larger massacres only a handful survived. Thousands fled to churches as places of sanctuary. But those churches, which in previous killings had been places of refuge, were this time just easy hunting grounds for the *interahamwe*. In Ruhanga, the people were gathered into the church and the pastor beheaded in front of his flock, then his family were burnt alive in their house. What followed was typical: grenades were thrown among the people, then they were shot. This reduced the thousands of people (at Ruhanga estimates vary between six and ten thousand) into a screaming, groaning mass of dead and dying, then the *interahamwe* would come with machetes and *impiris* (large clubs studded with nails).

Out of thousands and sometimes tens of thousands, survivors numbered less than double figures. At Nyarubuye estimates vary, but probably around ten thousand were killed. Some wounded survivors, their wounds festering with maggots, lay among the rotting bodies for over a month before being found. At Murambi, where between forty and fifty thousand people were surrounded and killed at a school compound, I met one of the four survivors six years after the massacre. He had been shot in the head and presumed dead, but managed to crawl away through the night before the bulldozers came to dispose of the bodies. It was clear the nightmare haunted him daily, his only request being for more money to keep drowning the pain in drink.

Aline's husband, parents and brothers and sisters were killed early in the genocide, but she hid in sorghum plantations with her four-month-old baby. 'The *interahamwe* came and used machetes to kill people,' said Aline. 'I was able to hide myself under the dead bodies with my baby. They stamped their feet on the bodies many times. After a week in those conditions RPF soldiers came and released us. My baby was severely sick because she was under the dead bodies and after a few days she died. Because I was hiding under the dead bodies that the interahamwe stamped on, I have cirrhosis and must take medicine, and I can only work a few days because of my disease.' Aline lived with the memories and nightmares of those days lying under bodies until she died in 2002, aged 29, from her injuries and sickness.

She was by no means the only person to survive in this way. In places there were piles of bodies up to ten deep, and with the killers roaming the fields and hills there was nowhere else to hide. Others were too badly injured to move, and lay where they were struck.

Odette Gahongayire, only fourteen at the time, spent the early days of the genocide hiding among the bushes as the *interahamwe* killed, burnt and looted. 'From wherever we were, we heard screams of people being killed; we saw blood flow like water and many other terrifying things.' Her father, brothers and more than thirty other people were forced into a house which was burnt down on top of them. Her mother was found and 'they hit her badly until blood and pus seeped out of her ears, nose and every outlet she had. When I found her she was breathing her last.'

When the *interahamwe* came to the family's banana plantation to look for food they found her hiding there and beat her until they thought she was dead. In excruciating pain she searched desperately for a place to hide. 'I went to hide in dead bodies. I smeared blood all over myself to hide my body. The dogs came to eat the bodies and if they found someone alive they barked and the *interahamwe* came and finished them off . . . I don't know how I managed to survive. I saw so many frightening evils, parents betraying their children, women being pounded to death, raped and many unspeakable things.'

When I was first introduced to the work of Solace, the first person I met who had survived under the bodies of others was a young boy who had fled to the top of a hill with his family until they had nowhere higher to run. Surrounded and defenceless, his family were mercilessly hacked to death. As they were knocked to the ground he was covered by a pile of dead relatives and survived unnoticed beneath the bodies. Night after night he relives the horror of wriggling out from the mutilated bodies of his dead family. Five years later he was virtually dumb, silenced into unremitting shock as the scene in his mind's eye ran through endless variations on what he had experienced.

At night, all over Rwanda, the last moments of their loved ones play themselves out on the hundreds of thousands of mental screens which are the memories of those who survived. Many survivors do not pass a night without bad dreams or insomnia, with the anniversary at the beginning of April intensifying the vividness of the nightmares. Some are unable even to lie down in bed. Chantal, one of the few survivors of Gikongoro, was still spending the night in bushes ten years after her traumatic experiences in 1994.

For those who survived, the nightmare that replays endlessly night after night is not just a visualisation in their sleep of what they experienced. It is often a dreadful recurring chase in which they struggle to flee machete-wielding *interahamwe*, and they wake up exhausted 'I saw the men who came to kill me with machetes,' described one survivor. 'I ran but they followed me until they killed me. I saw how I lay down on the ground, my head was cut. It was hard in my nightmare. When I woke up I was very afraid.' Many had to hide in the swamps and now experience a nightly desperate struggle as the swamp sucks them back into the hands of the killers.

The appalling visions are etched on the survivors' minds by their awful intensity. Sometimes the reality becomes hard to separate from the dream. One widow, Asterie, tells how she took hold of her husband's photograph to look at and suddenly found him standing in front of her. The imprinted trauma leapt out to become a shocking hallucination before her. After the genocide many children would cry hysterically for fear in broad daylight, 'seeing' attackers coming to kill them and their families.

Although the demonic blood-thirst enabled many of the general population to commit atrocious deeds, there are many who wish they could wind the clock back and live those months again. The faces of their victims pleading for mercy, the vicious wounds they inflicted, the whole spectacle of fear and pain they caused with their own hands has become a horror film playing repeatedly in their guilt-ridden minds.

Those who lost family and have never found their remains dream restlessly about their loved ones' end. Sakina Denise's husband was killed in Cyangugu, far from home, and never found. Like many others Denise clung to a forlorn hope he might have survived; such hope stubbornly refuses to disappear, especially as people are still being reunited many years after the genocide. For Denise the recurrent dream is being told her husband is alive and well, holding down a job in a building company and living without her. It makes no sense, but the absence of a burial plays many tricks on survivors' minds. Jacqueline from Gikongoro, whose husband was a driver, goes down the road day after day, year after year, to see if her husband is driving one of the trucks passing by.

Others who fled from attackers and were unable to help all their family flee are wracked by guilty nightmares in which they are accused of betrayal. Paul Gashumba ran from the killers with two children on his back. He still remembers the cries of anguish of his other four, who believed their father was abandoning them. There was nowhere to hide, and though they ran they were all killed. In his heart, he can still hear their desperate pleas for help. Donatilla tells how she had to leave her baby on the ground and flee for her life just after discovering the baby was dead. She was unable to make her way back to her baby, and struggled hard to overcome dreams of her baby still being alive and falling into the hands of the *interahamwe*.

Some of those who were very young at the time of the genocide remember little consciously but suffer vivid flashbacks. Bernadette Mukamunana* lost her mother, father and three siblings in the killing. She was four when the *interahamwe* came and multiple-raped her, infecting her with HIV. Bernadette often asks her sister about things that she can only vaguely remember, but as the years passed by she started to experience 'flashes of what happened to me or what I saw happening to others.' Those flashbacks come without warning and with fearsome vividness.

The reality of those dreams and nightmares is caught with stunning force by Job (7:13-15). Although placing the blame for his nightmares on God, his description of the results of such nightly torment is vivid: 'If I say, "My bed will comfort me, My couch will ease my complaint," then you frighten me with dreams and terrify me by visions; so that my soul would choose suffocation, death rather than my pains.' Imagine your worst ever nightmare and imagine dreaming it night after night, month after month for many years. And imagine waking up every morning to be reminded it is true.

For the nightmares to cease or diminish, the trauma of a survivor has to be addressed. When the soul begins to experience the healing of the cross, there is a freedom to begin unburdening the anger and unforgiveness. Healing flows, and the feelings of guilt, fear, sorrow and helplessness lessen.

Giving people practical help in rebuilding their homes, helping with income generation, or medical treatment for rape-induced HIV/AIDS, loosens the stranglehold of the nightmares by giving hope to the survivor. Every building block testifies that the future is worth living and the past is receding; and frees the mind from images of a tragic past and fears for a hopeless future.

Others require considerable ministry, and Christian counsellors note big differences between those who have accepted Christ and those who haven't. The emphasis is on the power of the blood of Jesus to wipe away the nightmare and for many definite release comes, though others find it hard to escape the nightly turmoil. They, especially, need continued love and prayer.

11

Reflections on Evil

There are many who have asked the question 'Why?' of the Rwandan genocide. It may be 'Why did God let it happen?', it may be 'Why did God not stop it?', it may be 'How can people do that to each other?' or it may be the far more desperate cry of a survivor: 'Why did that happen to me and my family?'

Those questions are asked by people everywhere after tragedy hits. People often want to blame God even though, before the tragedy, he was relegated to the side-lines of their lives. Why, when God is so regularly ignored, should he be blamed for his non-intervention?

There are complex reasons for ethnic conflict and genocide, and various writers have given excellent analyses. In his book *Triumph to Tragedy* Frank Retief, writing of a massacre in the church he pastored in South Africa, explained: 'The world is a place of tribulation and suffering. The suffering endured by Christians may at times take the form of persecution, but by and large it is part of the "showers of sorrow" that are the lot of all.'[31] The testimony of many whose stories are recorded here is that God in his grace stepped into the mêlée of human depravity and delivered, rescued and protected certain of his children, supernaturally blocking disaster which seemed inevitable.

Despite their religious cloak, the Rwandan people, including many in the church, had relegated God to the margins. The church failed to speak with any prophetic clarity into the injustice, hatred and sin that had penetrated much of the religious machinery and the nation. There was little of God's passionate concern for the poor manifest among the larger denominations, and even among some evangelical churches. There was little in the way of a prophetic voice regarding the massive problems of ethnic division, the refugees in Uganda and the growing polarisation of Rwandan society. And there was little apparent desire to tackle the problem of sin and compromise in the church. Of course within the church some individuals and even congregations strove diligently and passionately with prayer, preaching and example against such a general malaise. But they were exceptional.

There are still those outside the church who complain that it is only interested in its own numerical and economic progress, and not in the needs of the survivors and the poor. It is an accusation that is true to some extent, but wonderfully refuted by the sacrificial love and giving of many Rwandan Christians.

In Romans 1 there is a passage that describes the withdrawal of God's gracious protection from the consequences of sin. The society that turns from God's truth would be 'given over' to the lusts of their hearts and a depraved mind. This is exactly what happened in Rwanda. In Romans, Paul predicts 'wickedness, murder, strife, malice'.

In her book *Rwanda – The Land God Forgot?*[32] Meg Guillebaud discusses a number of issues that contributed to the genocide – among them the lack of discipling in the churches. There are many godly church leaders in Rwanda who point to this as a key weakness before the genocide. Perhaps there was a lack of biblical teaching covering lifestyle, relationship and attitudes, as preached by Jesus and the New Testament writers.

There is a saying in Rwanda that the church is 'many kilometres wide but few kilometres deep.' Two extremes were common, the first being evangelism which emphasised initial response but provided inadequate follow-up. Rubagumya, who leads a youth healing and reconciliation group in Kigali, points to the state of the church before 1994 and says most Christianity was nominal: 'People didn't get good teaching, and they were not rooted in the word of God. So a bad government was able to put ideas into people's minds, and both Christians and non-Christians accepted them.'

The second tendency, especially in the extremely large established church sector, was a contentedness to educate in sacrament and ritual, without ensuring that the word of God was changing the lives of members and adherents. It is said that 90 to 95 per cent of Rwandans profess to be Christian, with over 60 per cent claiming to be Roman Catholics, and with large Anglican and Adventist representations. However some church leaders, including the late David Ndaruhutse of African Revival Ministries, estimated that only about 8 per cent of Rwandans were born-again. The number of truly born-again Christians who were involved in the genocide was small, with some selflessly risking their own lives to save those of the other tribe. Some, however, were swept up by fear, peer pressure, or unresolved ethnic or personal grudges.

Many nominal church members, as well as priests and church leaders, have been implicated in the genocide, and indeed had a personal history of stirring up hatred and racial tension before the genocide began. Daphrose Kandanga* is one of the few survivors from Bisesero, and remembers how a Roman Catholic priest 'organised a meeting and asked all the people to send every Tutsi to hide in the church. They made them believe they would be safe there, but that was a lie because they had agreed that once in the church, not a single one would be spared. No one survived there.' She also recalls how on 14 April, just a few days later, 'soldiers spent all the day shooting at the Mugonero Hospital and Pastor [name supplied] led them. He is now in America. His son was with him killing people.'

There are those in the Rwandan church who have concerns today that new problems are replacing old ones. They are worried about the abundance of teaching that promises prosperity and puts too heavy an emphasis on prophecy at the expense of discipling hearts and lives with the Word. They want the spiritual fire, but are concerned there may be slovenliness in teaching and preaching which is covered up by fine-sounding exposition. There needs to be more prophetic 'wheat' and less 'chaff' (Jer. 23:28). God wants to raise the poor and meet their needs, but the gospel can easily look like a fast track to western materialism.

Paul Ndahigwa of *L'Église Vivante* has outlined six priorities for the church in the post-genocide era:

1. Transformed, committed Christians who have come into a real relationship with Christ and not with a religion
2. Christians who impact society by practising what they are taught in day-to-day life and demonstrating the power of the gospel to change lives
3. Christians who patiently strive to see unity in the body of Christ, complement one another in their gifts, and oppose competition and division

4. A better understanding of the word of God, and the establishment of consistent training for church leaders and workers
5. Evangelists who reach the entire nation with the uncompromising full gospel of our Lord Jesus Christ
6. Youth who are equipped with all the skills they need to build the nation, rather than being a negative force as they were in the genocide

The ferocity and cruelty of the genocide have led many, including the commander of the UN forces, to describe the element of demonic power in the genocide. Sonya Mukasekuru was ten years old at that time. When the killers came to her family, she escaped but returned to find a pile of dead and dying bodies in the house. She retrieved the head of her father and placed it beside the rest of his body before hiding behind a bed on which her mother lay severely wounded. As often happened, groups of killers returned to houses to finish people off. They cut her brother open and pulled out his intestines, then forced them into the mouth of his mother, declaring that she was only fit to drink the blood of her own children. Already greatly weakened, she died from the shock. Such behaviour has all the hallmarks of the devil at work.

But even if we agree that there was demonic activity during the genocide, that does not remove responsibility from the perpetrators. Demonic activity requires access to the life it uses. We don't fully know Judas's motives, but it seems he was not suddenly set upon by Satan: he went through a process of complaining, disillusionment, bitterness, greed, and allowing his heart to be taken over by evil (Jn.12:1-8, 13:2) before Satan entered him (Jn.13:27). Jealousy, hatred and bitterness were given a long and deep reign in the hearts of many

Rwandans before Satan had the opportunity to turn these impulses into genocide.

There is a further reason why demonic activity may have had access to some Rwandans, and provoked murder. In Rwandan folklore there is a being known as *Ryang'ombe* whose father was king of the *imandwa*, which are the higher echelon of spirits in Rwandan animist belief and have almost exclusively evil characteristics. They can only be placated through rituals performed out of fear. The stories involving *Ryang'ombe* are generally full of bloodshed and gratuitous killing. The worship and rituals associated with this belief include practising as a medium and possession by spirits. At the time of the genocide perhaps thirty per cent of Rwandans were involved at some level in the cult, including some Christians who mixed animist and Christian beliefs. During the rituals tribute is given to *Ryang'ombe* and during the colonial years, when tribal inequality became embedded in Rwanda, a form of protest by Hutu peasantry against Tutsi overlordship became part of the ritual. It appears that spirit possession, combined with the inherent anti-Tutsi nature of the ritual and its violent content, laid a foundation for the demonic inspiration of genocidal killing.

Even when people have made some kind of Christian profession, as with Simon of Samaria (Acts 8:9-24), a lack of true repentance and a continued desire for power rather than purity can cause someone to remain a captive of sin and influenced by their demonic past. A lack of true repentance, combined with evil forces being active in one's life, open the way for demonic activity to strengthen the hatred so that it becomes obsessively hateful and violent. Ephesians 4:27 clearly states: 'Do not give the devil a place.'

When demonic activity is mentioned in regard to the genocide, there is a tendency to assign to it an implication of guiltlessness on the part of the individual committing the act. For example, reporting on the massacre at Nyarubuye church, BBC reporter Fergal Keane records a *genocidaire* blaming Satan and adds that this was 'a common theme among the prisoners. Responsibility is passed out of their hands to some supernatural force. There are no guilty men, only victims of dark forces.'[33] This is a fair accusation to make against those perpetrators of genocide who hide behind Satan as the cause of their acts. However, a person has to present themselves as an instrument of unrighteousness for spiritual enslavement to result, and an act of obedience to that unrighteousness is required. Compulsion by the violence that led to genocide began as obedience to the bitterness, jealousy and hatred that separated people because of their tribes. The ability of demonic forces to capitalise on this does not excuse those involved, it simply indicates how completely they gave themselves up to evil.

Whatever the devil has done in Rwanda, the church has awoken to its call, and its responsibility to preach the true gospel of love and to disciple more effectively. John-Peter Gakwaya, vice-President of a healing and reconciliation group, was once committed to gaining revenge against the Hutus; but after the genocide he was saved and forgave those who had beaten and excluded him. 'The government has set the framework for unity,' he observes, 'but the church can reach the hearts.'

12

The Forgotten People

The genocide left huge numbers of children orphaned. In 1995 it was estimated that 875,000 children under fifteen in Rwanda had lost one or both parents. Not all were lost because of the genocide; illness and AIDS combined with the killing to leave about 30 per cent of children under fifteen with one or no parents.[34] Estimates of the number of child-headed households vary from ten thousand to a hundred and twenty thousand. A figure of forty-two thousand families headed by children, given by UNICEF[35] in 2001, may be a reasonable estimate. Children of ten, eleven and twelve had to look after themselves and younger brothers, sisters and cousins. Many families took in bereaved relatives but the scale of the problem overwhelmed the country's ability to absorb its consequences.

Damascene Kayiranga's father was killed, his mother and sister raped and killed, and he survived with two siblings by hiding in caves and bushes. At twelve years old, he found himself in a camp for displaced people with his younger brother and sister to look after. 'We had a terrible time to survive,' he says

No one cared for us as we had no uncles, aunts or other relatives. They were all killed. We used to beg for food and very often had none at all. We couldn't pay the rent of the slum we were in and kept crying to God, who helped us. When we went back to our home area people mocked us, saying, 'Look at those cursed Tutsi with no one to look after them.' We started to plough our own land and because our house was destroyed and we were staying in a ruin, it fell down. We went back to Kigali and were given a house in an orphan settlement, but that one fell down as well. Now we live in another slum and finding food is difficult, so we often go several days without eating. It is a miracle, because when we are starving God uses people to give us food.

Not only did those children face the practical challenge of finding food and shelter for themselves and their dependants, they also carried massive psychological, emotional, social and spiritual wounds. Hundreds of thousands of children were now growing up with no recognisable authority figure in their lives, and no one to teach them how to parent their younger brothers and sisters or even look after themselves. Very quickly they lost their childhood, and with it their schooling which they gave up to look after their siblings. Teenage girls were sometimes harassed sexually in their new vulnerability, food and protection being offered in exchange for sexual favours, and pregnancy in their young teenage years was sometimes the result. Others had been raped and were suffering from HIV/AIDS. Many children ended up in the streets.

Constance Kayitesi was born in 1984 and was the eldest of six children. She lived in south-west Rwanda in the province of Gitarama, but by school age she had moved to stay with an aunt in Kigali to help with her schooling. She describes her early years: 'I started there in the primary school, and when I was in my third year of primary the genocide started. I was ten years old.' As you read what follows, remember that. Think of a ten-year-old girl you know. Now Constance is tall, almost six feet, with fine smooth features, and her long neck and good looks accentuate her beauty. But then she was just a little girl.

It was 7 April 1994 and Constance suddenly found herself surrounded by *interahamwe* and other killers at her aunt's home. Her aunt was away at Kibungo, a town about one hundred kilometres to the south-east. Only Constance and a girl looking after her were at home. The killers wanted Constance's aunt, and speaking with cold menace they issued the simple promise that Constance should tell her aunt they will come back and kill her. Suddenly feeling dreadfully isolated from her family and sure that death awaited her, she decided to go back home and die with her parents.

Caught between moments of fear and hope, Constance told her aunt: 'Maybe my father will be stronger than the killers and will fight and win against them.' She set off home. There was a long way to go, perhaps thirty miles, and she had to avoid the roadblocks already springing up all round Kigali. For twenty miles Constance dodged the killers, but there was no way over the Nyabarongo River except by a manned bridge. It is a tributary of the Nile, and the extremist Hutu ideology has established a myth that the Tutsis really belong in the north, further down the river. Already people had been killed and thrown into it to take them back down the Nile.

Constance remembered both Rwandan and white soldiers there, but who the white soldiers were she had no idea. She tried to avoid their stare, but one of the

Rwandan soldiers suddenly exclaimed: 'Look at that *akanyenzi*!' An akanyenzi is a small inyenzi, a cockroach. He wanted to kill her, but perhaps the presence of the white soldiers compelled him to let her go and be killed by others.

Near the settlement of Ruyenzi Constance stumbled into a roadblock commanded by a woman. She played a cruel joke on Constance, mocking her height as a Tutsi. 'If you're taller than the roadblock we'll kill you, but if you're smaller we'll let you go,' she laughed. The roadblock came up to Constance's thigh. They shouted at her to sit down on the road to be killed. She felt so helpless, so scared, but the militia surrounded her and there was no possibility of escape. Just seconds from the lethal slash of the machete, a loud noise erupted nearby. Some *interahamwe* were looting a house of those they'd killed and making a lot of noise about it. Those at the roadblock were more interested in the possibility of loot than another victim, and ran to where the noise was coming from. No one wanted to be left out and Constance suddenly found herself unguarded. She ran for her life.

Near her home village the work of the *interahamwe* was evident and the smell of death filled the air. Houses all around were broken down; the work had been swift and she was temporarily disorientated. She was sure she was home but looked around to check her bearings, which confirmed that the pile of rubble on the ground was all that remained of her house.

There was no one around and confusion filled her heart, but there was nothing else to do but keep walking. There were people she knew at Mugina, and she turned east and started off again. Constance showed amazing endurance, travelling dozens of miles over this country of a thousand hills, with no food to eat and no one to help her. But nothing prepared her for Mugina, where thirty thousand people had rushed into the church compound believing themselves to be safe in a 'holy' place. When the *interahamwe* arrived there were too many tightly-packed people for them to kill. They surrounded the compound for several days until the terrified Tutsis were weakened by lack of food and water. By the time Constance arrived there was a sea of bodies littering the ground, a reality too terrible for her ten-year-old understanding to take in. A survivor broke the news that her aunt, uncle and grand-mother were dead. She was utterly lost, without protection, without family, without home.

She describes what happened next. 'I stayed there for thirty minutes, walking about looking for other people I knew among the bodies.' There were babies desperately suckling at the dry breasts of their dead mothers. Some survivors were groaning and crying out, unable to move because of their injuries, many with tendons on their legs cut through with machetes to stop them leaving. Constance heard laughing and shouting, and a group of *interahamwe* came to finish off those who were still breathing. She was dangerously close to being seen and captured. 'I ran towards a bush and they didn't see me,' she says. 'Then I decided to go to Kabgayi.' It was still the rainy season, with ferocious thunderstorms. 'I had to spend nights in the bush, sometimes in the rain. I knew there were people who had gone to Kabgayi and I was sure no one would come to kill people inside the bishop's compound.' She was desperately mistaken: Kabgayi was another area where mass killings took place.

On the way she had to cross a bridge guarded by militiamen. The previous scene of humiliation was repeated with the jibes at her height and the hopeless measurement, and this time it came up to her chest. There was no diversion this time, and they beat Constance with wooden clubs studded with nails, raining down blows on her. Another group of Tutsis were beaten too, including a mother and baby. The *interahamwe* killed the woman and watched, laughing, as the baby cried for her mother. Then they killed the baby too, and threw both bodies in the river.

A car full of Presidential Guards arrived and they cheered on the *interahamwe*, some of them joining in. Constance's young body could take no more and she passed out. This saved her, as the killers could see no signs of life and left her for dead. Gradually Constance regained consciousness and limped down to the river to wash. There was no help, no doctors, no painkillers. She had no option but to keep stumbling on, looking for someone she knew to find shelter with.

A man approached. He seemed concerned at Constance's condition and asked what had happened. Constance remembers the conversation: 'I told him I was going to Kabgayi and had been beaten by bad people. He offered to take me to his house so that he could try and heal me. My wounds had gone septic and I could not move my head.'

The man knew she needed to go to hospital but her clearly Tutsi features made it hazardous. He took her to St Joseph's, a school at Kabgayi, and left her in the care of a priest who assured him she would be safe. For a moment things took a turn for the better. Amongst the many refugees she was amazed to find some survivors from her family, including her father, an aunt and two younger sisters.

But shortly after she arrived there was an ominous development. The *interahamwe* surrounded the school and cut off the water supply. Apparently a woman army major was angry that there were 'still cockroaches alive'. Soon afterwards soldiers started to enter the compound with buses, which they filled with refugees and drove away. Constance would find out later that there were no survivors from those buses. They came back empty and were filled again. The third time, her father was one of those forced to board a bus.

He had guessed what was happening and refused and started to struggle, whereupon the soldiers beat him with a gun until he fell down and could not stand again. Some boys standing nearby were made to carry him on to the bus, then forced on themselves. Constance could only watch helplessly: everywhere soldiers controlled the refugees. The situation continued for the next few days while Constance was still with her two sisters and her aunt. There was nothing to eat, the water had run out, and they watched helplessly as the life of her baby sister Nyiranuma faded and she finally died.

Suddenly there was the sound of gunfire. Minutes later the soldiers disappeared and the compound was taken by RPF soldiers.

Much later, Constance was taken in by her aunt who had survived in Kibungo. Her brothers had fled to Congo and also survived, and amazingly only one of the six children had died. But they were now orphans, and deeply traumatised by the horrors of the last three months.

Things got worse when the aunt got married and her husband began to beat Constance and the other children. 'He said we couldn't continue to live with him, as all we did was consume things without bringing anything in.' She was going to secondary school, but her aunt's husband was abusing her and the others. She found it hard to keep going, and has painful memories of the low days: 'Sometimes I felt I wanted to hang myself and die. Then I remembered that I was the elder and that my brothers and sisters had their eyes on me.'

Constance's road to healing began when she was in her second year at secondary school. 'I had a lot of deep sorrow in my heart, and I thought my life was finished and it would be better if I died. After I lost my parents, life was not worth anything any more. I didn't feel I could do anything for myself, so how could I help the others?'

In Rwanda there are so many widows and orphans who find no purpose in their lives. The pain has been knocked into their heart so hard that there is nothing left to live for. Many wish they had not survived. The distress is worse, they say, for those left than for those who died. The preaching and teaching that is given to orphans and widows starts with their survival: God must mean them to live.

At that time church was not on Constance's agenda. 'I felt really discouraged and did not like church because I felt God had abandoned us. I also felt it was not safe in church because so many were killed there.' But there were some other children in her class at school who began to tell her about Jesus, and Constance realised if she was spared then maybe God had a purpose for her. But like many children subjected to abuse and trauma, she could only blame herself for what had happened: 'When I started to think about God I thought God would not hear me because I counted myself a terrible sinner.' The schoolmates led her to the Lord, and 'I found that I cannot have peace anywhere except in God alone.'

Some of her brothers and sisters had also given their lives to Christ, but Constance's recovery had only just begun. She went to a large association of survivors in Rwanda but, overwhelmed with requests, they could not help. However, their President gave her the phone number of the Christian organisation, Solace Ministries.

For Constance it was like stumbling on an oasis in the desert. At last she had found a place to unburden her soul. 'I went to Solace Ministries and they received me,' she says. 'I was astonished at how they listened to me carefully with love and compassion.' She doesn't need to tell you she has peace because you can see it in her eyes. She is mindful to thank God. 'I can tell you now that I have peace because I have the source of peace and even those who have parents do not have peace like me, because I have the most important Parent.'

Psalm 68:5 says: 'A father of the fatherless and a judge for the widows, is God in His holy habitation.' Many thousands of orphans like Constance have endured terrible pain, awful nightmares, poverty and hunger, with no father or mother to comfort them. God has filled this void.

God's grace continued to work in Constance's life. Her aunt's husband evicted her, but Solace Ministries bought a three-room house for her and six dependent relatives. The house is mud-brick with a cement coating, and the family work hard at its upkeep. However, they had no income and were surviving on occasional bowls of sorghum porridge The youngest, Candida, was one year old at the time of the genocide and survived by being fed milk by a kindly Catholic nun, but now she is reaching up towards six feet like the rest of the family. In a partnership between Solace and a Scottish charity, Comfort Rwanda, child-headed households are now being sponsored as whole families. Constance and her family are among them.

As Constance speaks there is a lightness and life in her voice. With renewed hope, her face breaks into a smile, revealing her white, bright teeth, as she speaks of God's protection over her life. Like many who had lost the will to live she used to find it hard even to look after her hair, but now it is combed down her long neck, wavy and healthy.

She hopes 'God will enable us to help others.' She is already working hard in her spare time to motivate other orphans and widows. Many other child-headed households have been inspired by her testimony, and become good examples for other survivors in Rwanda. Her life is a wonderful example of how to respond to the gospel with faith and hope.

Constance's story is not yet finished. Now aged twenty-three, she awaits her secondary exam results to see if she can go to university. If her marks are high enough she will get a scholarship. Otherwise she needs to find £600. At present, through sponsorship, she receives £34 a month to live on with seven others. Freeing herself from the cycle of poverty will be a long struggle.

Apart from 'being a mother to the family', she wants to become an electronic engineer. Many children from child-headed households fail to get good marks at school because of their responsibilities at home, but she needs those high marks for the scholarship She is undaunted by the challenge ahead. Constance has found that with God all things are possible. The future may be tough, but it has lost its power to keep her fearful and hopeless.

She laughs, smiles and hugs with gratitude to God for his goodness, and with genuine joy and peace in her heart. It's an infectious joy amid the pain and sorrow of Rwanda.

13

Saved for a New Generation

Ben Kayumba has dedicated his life to bring healing to the broken survivors of 1994, and to inspire a new generation of youth who will never repeat the evil of 1994. He is another who has chosen to serve survivors by God's direction, embodying the words of comfort in Isaiah 61:1-4. It hasn't been an easy ride for Ben: the choices have been difficult and there has been a high cost to pay. Ben was working for Compassion International when the genocide erupted, but his life hung in the balance five weeks before the main killing began. After the murder of Bucyana Martin, the President of the Hutu extremist CDR party, near where Ben lived, the *interahamwe* surrounded all the nearby Tutsis and started to kill them. Only a last-minute phone call to a Belgian contact, who managed to persuade the UN to rescue Ben with a lightning operation involving jeeps and machine guns, saved his life. It is amazing how the peace of God can overcome the most fearful of situations.

'I was surrounded by *interahamwe* about to kill me,' explains Ben, 'but I felt the voice of God say: "Don't fear, you will be rescued", and I felt great peace and not fear.

Immediately after that the phone went to tell me help was on the way.'

During the genocide Ben tried to escape to Burundi, but thousands were being stopped at the roadblocks and killed. Again God spoke to Ben and told him: 'Don't be afraid, be ready to cross the border tonight.' Immediately a taxi driver friend arrived and Ben crossed into Burundi without a passport. Despite those words of God he was deeply shocked. His mother, father and more than two hundred cousins, aunts, uncles and immediate family had all been killed, and he began to show symptoms of breakdown. The next hurdle was to get a passport, and God worked in the ambassador's heart to grant him a free one. 'God has told me you are going to give me a passport,' Ben told the ambassador. Tutsi refugees were just not in the running for passports from the Hutu Rwandan ambassador in Burundi. 'People were so amazed he gave me a passport, they thought I must be a spy!' remembered Ben.

In Burundi, a businessman bought a ticket for him to fly to Uganda where he met Jacques Masiko, the director of Compassion in Uganda, and his staff. One of those he met was a man called Dan Brewster, who said to Ben: 'I have a word from God for you – you are to go back to Rwanda.' Ben spent the next two days praying and seeking confirmation from the Lord. 'God spoke to me and said: "I saved you for a purpose. You are to go and help orphans and widows. The choice you have to make is to go back, and I will protect you."' It was a hard choice but Ben broke the news to Compassion, with tears running down his face: he would indeed go back into Rwanda immediately.

Compassion had gathered considerable funds to tackle the Rwandan crisis and Ben remembers well the vast challenge but wonderful fulfilment of helping people in the most desperate need. The RPF were very wary of allowing aid organisations into territory they held, but Ben was not to be turned back. 'I have suffered more than you, let us use the money here. I have survived and I am not to go away from Rwanda but I am to help my nation and those who have survived like me, as God instructed me,' he told them. 'God empowered me and they gave me permission for six months, five months more than they would even give well known international aid organisations.' By 12 May, just over thirty-five days into the hundred days of genocide, Ben was back in Rwanda.

In August 1995 he travelled to the Congo with Rob Davis of Compassion Rwanda, to meet other staff in exile after the genocide. Even there he was not safe, as some bishops who could have saved his parents during the killing were travelling around trying to raise money to arm the militias and re-attack Rwanda. They identified Ben and once again his life was in the balance. But God's Spirit was in him and with great boldness he prophesied to the bishops that God would foil them and bring healing to the nation. Their plans were thwarted and Ben went free. His account of those many escapes from death recalls the people of Nazareth, filled with rage, leading Jesus to the brow of a hill to throw him down the cliff, 'but passing through their midst, He went His way.' Such deliverance arms Ben with a powerful message for those who survived because he knows that survival is for a purpose.

The healing of Ben's trauma came in two stages. To begin with, very quickly, God restored him sufficiently to begin looking after survivors, especially orphans. It was a one-off direct touch from God which suddenly removed the fear and pain. Ben set up eight orphanages and displaced people camps, rising to the challenge with the passion of one who knew it was God's time for his life to bear fruit. When he managed to return to his home village, there was nothing to be found but broken homes and 567 decapitated heads.

In 1995, friends in Canada had Ben to stay and the agony resurfaced. He was offered a life with a beautiful home near Calgary. 'I wept and mourned and felt very weak and distressed,' Ben recalls. He grieved for his lost family members, he wept at the atrocities he had seen, and he shook at the thought of the many times he had been threatened and narrowly avoided death. In particular, he mourned his fiancée who had been killed. But God spoke to Ben again: 'I have a mission for you: you need to look after the survivors, your family, the widows and orphans of Rwanda and the church.' Once again Ben responded to God's call and returned to Rwanda. 'My friend said to me "I think you're stupid" and was angry with me, but I knew it was God's voice I'd heard. I know my experience of the genocide and my willingness to heed God's voice was challenging him, and later he got properly saved and became a pastor.'

As Ben arrived at the small airport in Kigali and the plane touched down, the peace of God descended. Once again God supernaturally healed his deep wounds, and he has never experienced such suffering again. The anointing of the Spirit for his work is very precious to Ben. 'When we minister to the survivors sometimes people need deliverance from demonic power; we can be affected and I can sometimes feel the demonic oppression and a reduction in power,' he explains. At such times the constant fight against evil can weaken those who minister like Ben and they are acutely aware of their need for the empowering of the Holy Spirit. Night and day they continue to counsel and minister and pray, and to bring freedom to the captives and the hurting.

This is the Kayumba (Ben's surname) of whom Donatilla spoke in her poem: 'May you always have Kayumba who swore not to sleep while others cannot sleep.' He looks at me with total sincerity and commitment and says: 'God is empowering me. I have my own weaknesses and strengths, but we have a destiny to bring healing to the widows and orphans.' It is a destiny being fulfilled every day.

Ben's wife Stephanie lost her first husband three days after she had given birth to their daughter, Diane. Due to Stephanie's trauma two weeks into the genocide, when she was hiding in an attic to escape the *interahamwe*, Diane was born a month prematurely. Stephanie's father and brothers were all killed, and Stephanie has found it hard to let the pain go. She is quiet and gentle but her thoughts run deep, and her inner hurt is taking a long time to heal. But sharing her pain has allowed the ministry of the cross access to her injured soul. Ben is sure that Diane too has been affected by the fear communicated to her when she was seven days old, as Stephanie escaped from the front lines of fighting between the RPF and government soldiers. There was an assault going on, with bombs and bullets landing all around them. 'It was very very frightening for her,' Ben says, 'and sometimes you can see Diane lapsing into silence and something is going on inside her.'

Each year Ben organises Solace Ministries youth camps for almost two thousand young people, most of them orphaned by the genocide. He has become 'Papa' to many of them and is dedicated to shaping their lives under the guidance of God for good. He and his co-workers counsel hundreds of children at those camps, helping them face the deeply buried memories of horrific experiences and the violent loss of parents and families. Through this counselling the survivors come to healing, forgiveness and wholeness in Christ.

Over 90 per cent of Rwandan youth saw a relative or
friend violently murdered. Lawrence Kajuga* recently
arrived at Solace. He was only seven years old during
the genocide. When a large group of Tutsis were shot he
was kneeling down tending his injured mother and survived because he was covered by the falling bodies. He
spent days hiding in the corpse-filled water channels of
the swamps before he was told his uncle had been found
alive. He found his father who had been crucified on a
tree then thrown off a hill into thorn bushes, where he
remained alive. Nails had been driven through him
down the length of his body and the flesh had started to
rot around the nails but Lawrence was unable to free
him and had to flee, leaving him to die.

The work of helping young people recover in the
healing camps continues. Healing and forgiveness are
important, and these children have no parents to help
them at school or show them how to live. The leaders
encourage them to work hard at school and many of the
orphans they work with are excelling in their studies,
unlike others who struggle with the weight of past hurts
and present responsibilities. For those who have no
funds there may have to be financial support for their
schooling and materials, about £100 a year being the difference between an uneducated future with limited
prospects or an education and a climb out of the poverty trap.

Ben talks often of 'generation transfer' to describe his
passion for a new cohort of godly young people: 'The
main evil came through the youth. The former government used the youth to indoctrinate them and train
them for the killing. Most of the killing was by the youth
and the whole generation was committed to evil.'
Today's young people in Rwanda are learning a different way. Ben is animated and passionate about their

potential: 'They are the generation of the future and our first responsibility is to change that history and give them hope for the future.' The mission is clear: to protect history by recording accurately the experiences during the genocide, to change history by creating a unified society, and to make the history of the future one of peace. Ben adds: 'It is the church in Rwanda that must own this vision and raise up godly youth. Please pray for this dream.'

The task is massive: to bring up the children of Rwanda in a different way, to break the decades-old cycle of hatred and retribution, and to create a new Rwanda. Many Christians have a deep sense that God has called them for such a time as this, and that they have a great responsibility to erase the shame of the church and take a front-line role in tackling the roots and results of the genocide. It is remarkable that God has given his church a second chance, a commission they are eager to fulfil graciously.

As Ben ministers to the young people of Rwanda today, he proclaims a particular message: 'We talk about the value of human beings made in the image of God'. Such a message provides a firm foundation for love. 'We also emphasise how to behave as godly people.' There is a seriousness to the preaching of the message, to the endless hours of counselling, teaching and training. Servants like Ben have a deep sense of calling and destiny, and they bear that calling with dignity, humility and tireless commitment. God is blessing their message of salvation, unity and godliness by inspiring thousands of young people with a passion for the glory of God.

Some of those young people in churches across the nation are forming healing and reconciliation groups. The leader of one such group outlines their aims for young people

- Establishing healing, unity and reconciliation in Rwanda
- Teaching people repentance and forgiveness at the cross
- Counselling those with broken hearts
- Teaching people to live in harmony
- Teaching poor people a skill

Perhaps for the first time in many decades in Rwanda, the church is beginning to disciple converts in principles of Christian living in a way that can provide a lead to the nation. Today's youth will form the society of tomorrow, and if young churchgoers truly receive the seed of the gospel of peace, the future for Rwanda will be strongly influenced by them. As many of the Christian youth say: 'We are from different tribes and different churches but we want to reach everyone and tell them what Jesus Christ has done for us.'

14

Supernatural Restoration

Ruth Mudenge* desperately needed healing. Her sad eyes have at last brightened from the healing touch of Jesus but it has been a difficult journey for this young woman who was wounded so deeply as a child. There was nothing in her early life that pointed to the tragic events that would burst upon her in later years. She speaks of a good life, Rwandan style. Although Rwanda is one of the most densely populated countries in Africa, big families are still applauded. Ruth's family was typically large – eight children, a dad who was a teacher, and mum who worked on the farm. For many in Rwanda one goat is a bonus but the family had goats, cows and hens.

The invasion of the north of Rwanda in 1990 came as a surprise to Ruth: her parents had taught her much, but not about the ethnic problems that plagued the country. When the RPF invaded and tensions rose, her father was arrested and accused of being an RPF accomplice. He was beaten and his arm broken so badly it took over a year to heal. For the children the harassment was constant: Ruth and her brothers and sisters were regularly beaten and stoned by Hutu children indoctrinated with the increasingly menacing anti-Tutsi propaganda prom- ulgated by the radio and encouraged in the schools.

Ruth's initiation into the horrors of genocide began when she was barely a teenager. One evening she went for food. She describes what happened: 'A government soldier arrested me and raped me. I was thirteen years old. It was terrible and very painful. I could not walk afterwards, and stayed where he raped me as I did not even want to go home and stayed outside overnight. My parents feared I was dead, but they found me in a trench near the road the following morning.'

Things continued to deteriorate when Ruth found she was pregnant from the rape. Her parents were in a tragic dilemma, driven to distraction by the plight of their daugh- ter. She was still at primary school, desperately young to bear a baby, and they were advised by friends to take her for an abortion. The family is Christian and her parents refused, deciding the right choice was to let the baby be born and entrust it to the care of nuns. It was a desperately hard choice but Ruth went through with the birth, handed the baby over to the nuns and returned to school.

As the persecutions intensified the family feared for its safety and decided to flee to the capital Kigali. Soon after- wards the persecution and maltreatment at the hands of the army, police and neighbours drove her father not just to sympathise with the RPF but to join them. There was a temporary increase in the hope for a cessation of vio- lence when a peace accord was signed in Arusha, Tanzania in late 1993. Ruth took back her one-year-old daughter Nadine from the nuns and her mother helped nurse her. The family sought to settle down to normal life while the father waited behind RPF lines as the truce temporarily held and Ruth, her mind whirling with the confusion and pain of recent events, attempted to pursue her studies.

It is 6 April 1994, and Ruth is sitting in her uncle's house. It is the school holiday and she is enjoying a break in Kigali, without baby Nadine, when news begins to break on the radio that the President's plane has crashed. Her uncle's family anxiously discuss the danger they are in. They wait in fear and the next evening they are gathered in the living room, hardly daring to move. The evening starts to cool and Ruth goes through to the bedroom to look for a warm shirt for her aunt's baby, Kalisa. At just that moment soldiers break into the house, and from her room she hears the sound of guns again and again. She throws herself under the bed and waits, heart pounding, listening, waiting. It is not until morning that she thinks it is safe to come out. Despite the shooting she has heard, it is still a severe shock to find the bodies of her uncle's family and her nine-month-old cousin, Kalisa,* sucking his dead mother's breast.

For five days she lives with the dead relatives lying in the living room, as there is nothing she can do to bury them and nowhere she can go in safety. Eventually she hears the *interahamwe* entering the house. Their careful administration of targeted homes and families has shown them the house is due for looting. Again she hides under the bed, hearing their shouts and laughter coming into the bedroom, and suddenly the mattress is pulled off and she lies motionless, exposed and helpless.

She is taken out with the baby and her relatives' bodies are quickly buried near the house. Nearby is a roadblock which doubles as a killing point but she is safe for the moment as the blood-sated killers debate her fate and decide to let her go to be killed elsewhere. There are some friends of her uncle's nearby and she makes for their house with Kalisa, but the family is too afraid of reprisals and refuse to take them in. She knows of an orphanage and asks for help, but is met by a woman who refuses her access and calls on a nearby soldier to kill her. 'You are from the Tutsis and God has abandoned the Tutsis,' she is told.

There is a deep pit latrine nearby, its cover ripped off, and she is dragged to the pit and ordered to throw Kalisa into the hole. She pleads for the child's life and the soldier seems weary with the slaughter and walks off, but the roadblocks are all around and there is nowhere to escape. They are stopped at another roadblock and she looks around and sees fourteen other women waiting to be killed. She is ordered to put the baby on the ground, strip and walk with the other women with their heads bent to their knees to a big hole dug near the roadblock.

One by one the women are pushed into the hole and killed. Paralysed by fear, Ruth waits her turn, but again she is rescued. There is a soldier of higher rank who says he wants to kill her himself. But somehow another man who knew her uncle arrives and she is taken to his home and given food and milk for the baby. Her life is marked by God for preservation, but the *interahamwe* have not finished their attempts to end it.

They are aware she has been saved and the next evening they come to the house and take her away, beating her with guns as she stumbles on. They make their way into a forest until they arrive at a small house in a clearing. Sensing her baby cousin Kalisa's life is also in danger she has left her at the edge of the forest. Ruth herself is pushed into the house and is met by a group of naked women and young girls brought from a nearby school. Her clothes are roughly removed and she is pushed on to the floor. There is a room set aside in the house and one by one the women and girls are taken into the room. They don't come back: unknown to Ruth there is a mass grave dug out at the back where the *inter-ahamwe* are disposing of the bodies.

As the women and girls are taken the rest are left wait-ing, but Ruth keeps turning to God and prays and prays. She is the twenty-fourth to be taken and remembers again the evil of that rape: 'There were two men inside. There was a plastic sheet with blood on it and they asked me to sit on it. They raped me and after that they obliged me to drink blood that was on the side of a small hoe. They killed people with that small hoe. They then pushed me in a hole and I fell on other bodies, some had died, some were still breathing.' Trembling naked on the bodies, she waits to be shot, but the noise of guns and mortars rapidly increases and her attackers suddenly turn and run. Mortars are falling all around as the RPF advance, and she is hit on the head by shrapnel. Time seems to have no relevance any more but it seems that the fighting flares all around her for a long time. She finds herself stuck in a pit full of bodies.

Ruth has deep reserves of faith and begins to pray intensely again – 'I prayed a lot,' – and Jesus steps down into the nightmare. There is someone coming very close wearing white clothes, bright shining white. She is struck forcibly by their brightness and her first confused thought is of her mother coming to rescue her. But this is not her mother, and the man in white puts a hand on her shoulder with great compassion and starts to speak, comforting her, encouraging her not to fear or worry because he is with her. He turns to go and Ruth asks him to stay: quietly he insists the time has not yet come and he goes. Is this Jesus? Filled with fear and confusion, she doesn't recognise him.

As he leaves, the sound of other voices increases and she guesses they are RPF soldiers. She is still down in the big hole amongst the bodies of the dead and dying, but the hole is too steep to climb out of and she shouts for help. Badly injured and weakened, she struggles to get out of the pit, slipping on the decaying bodies. One of the soldiers has to jump in to help push her out and at last she is carried off to safety, but the battle is fierce all around them and the soldiers have to leave her in the wood and fight on. Again she is visited by the man in white and he begins to comfort her. He tells her clearly that her time is not yet but she will once again come through this adversity. She needs the comfort and help because the soldiers have forgotten about her, and only come back when their commander asks where the girl they rescued has gone.

The end of the genocide was not the end of the suffering, and Ruth recalls the pain of the following years: 'There were only five of us, whereas we used to be ten; my mother and four brothers and sisters had been killed. I was always sick and crying. My father did all he could for me; he brought me to different hospitals but when we learned that I had been infected with AIDS, he wept and fell in deep sorrow. After the school began, I started to get used to my disease.' As for baby Kalisa, she was found in the forest by a neighbour and survived to be reunited with Ruth.

As the years passed the family found the pain, the loss and the illness hard to cope with. The father decided to marry a Hutu woman but they broke up again soon after. Ruth describes how her mental health deteriorated and she became 'crazy'. Life continued to spiral downward when she tried unsuccessfully to drown herself in the Nyabarongo River but was taken by another soldier, raped again and once more made pregnant. 'I felt I was walking dead,' she says.

Her father tried marriage again, to another woman who had no love for the children, and they had to split up and find surviving relatives to live with. Ruth went to live with her aunt in Nyamirambo and there were thirteen children all together there, all orphans. Her aunt had no child of her own and it was a heavy burden for her to find food and provide for them. Ruth's health deteriorated, skin diseases appeared, her weight kept going down and she hid herself away. She had been reunited with the child of her first rape and says: 'I was very deeply depressed. I hated God, the Hutu and the child I bore. I was very, very desperate.'

Because of her experiences she lived with a constant fear of Hutu men, always believing they intended to take her again and rape her. The fear was worsened because some of those she knew had been involved in the genocide were still at liberty. It was hard to live with the pain of her trauma and meet some of those who had not yet been indicted by international or local judiciaries. The injustice of her situation would hit hard at such times.

The depression and shame almost kept her from hope. A girl called Angelique had been to one of the Solace Ministries trauma healing camps, and having been greatly helped she began to share with Ruth what she had experienced. But Ruth was so disgusted with life, people and herself that at first she refused to grasp the possibility of hope. Angelique's insistence had an effect on Ruth's aunt, who visited Solace and poured out the story of her family. The healing of God began to restore her, and she pleaded with Ruth to visit Solace. 'I only wanted death,' she says, 'and I kept refusing to go.'

Ruth's conflict was both with herself and with God. 'I had such a strong inner conflict,' she says. But with God there was both disillusionment and confusion. 'I always wanted to ask him: "Where were you when the baby was breastfeeding on his dead mother? Where were you when this soldier took me in 1992 and raped me? Where were you when all these people at my uncle's were shot dead? Where were you when we were in a queue of many women, waiting naked to be thrown in that mass grave near Baobabin Nyamirambo? Where were you . . .?"'

At last she gave in to her aunt and decided to visit Solace. When she arrived, she made her position very clear to Jean Gakwandi, who spoke with her. 'Before we talk let me tell you three things: do not ask me to love God, because he rejected me; do not ask me to love the Hutus, because they made of me what I am today; and do not ask me to love the child that was born to me through the rape. I hate her.' She remembers with a wry smile the way she spoke to him: 'I was not very kind to them because I felt angry. Not against them, perhaps. But only angry.'

'I gave her the opportunity to express herself in the way she wanted and listened to her from 10.00 a.m. to 1.00 p.m., non-stop,' remembers Jean. 'I found in her a person who has really suffered but who has never had an opportunity to be understood and comforted, and then we prayed.' The warmth of God's love, through his people, overwhelmed her immediately. The self-loathing, fear and shame melted and she felt a great sense of relief, and a new sense of her own value: 'They made me feel I was worth something and was not just a piece of garbage.'

For eleven years she had not believed anyone could care enough to help, to listen, to love – not to turn away but to be genuinely concerned about her. Now at last the pain could find a way out.

It was later, in May 2005, that God restored her. She had started attending the meetings at Solace and the hatred she felt in her heart for God was beginning to break. While the widows and orphans were worshipping and praising God, the Spirit came down upon her. The joy of the Lord flooded her soul and began to rise up and overflow. She was weak from AIDS, but her feet found strength and she began to dance before God: 'I started to dance because of the joy that came in my heart. I started to praise God and to thank him. I started to feel that I love the people I hated before.'

Suddenly a picture of 1994 came racing back. This time it wasn't the faces of evil killers or the shocking nightmares of atrocities and mass graves. It was someone in white with beautiful, bright, clean white garments. Someone who loved her very much and put his hand on her shoulder and never left her. 'I know now it was Jesus who came to me,' she says with a smile. 'I know that I survived as a miracle.'

For someone who has endured the horrors Ruth Mudenge has, the most protracted and intensive trauma therapy would be needed, but the supernatural touch of God provides restoration for the heart and soul. 'He heals the broken-hearted and binds up their wounds' (Ps. 147:3) and 'The Lord is near to the broken-hearted and saves those who are crushed in spirit' (Ps. 34:18) is how the Bible describes it. 'I do not understand what happened really – I feel I am a new person,' is how Ruth explains it. 'I can talk with people and I have no feeling of hatred and resentment any more. I love God so deeply. I remember the man in white who found me in the pit with dead bodies and in the wood and I believe it is Jesus. I have peace.'

The transformation is remarkable for the fruit it has produced in her relationship with Nadine, her daughter born from the first rape. She had breast-fed her second child born from rape, and a maternal bond had grown between them, but she had hated her first-born daughter for almost fourteen years. When she was saved her heart was completely changed: she found the hatred replaced by love, and the hostility gave way to the tenderness of a mother. 'She is a new person to me. I love her and when she comes to me I feel motherly tenderness. I believe it is because of Jesus. She did not do any wrong at all.' Her main concern is the amount of time she has been spending in hospital, the effect of the years of separation on Nadine, and her inability to provide for her because of her lack of money.

Despite her poor health, Ruth has begun to live a life of thanks and praise, and to testify about Jesus. After years of fighting AIDS her slim body is fragile, but her face shines with the glory of God. Gakwandi describes her as 'a real woman of God': her life is devoted to finding enough strength to visit other sufferers to tell them of the good news in Jesus. She has often said she could die at any moment, but now she has peace. Her home situation has certainly not been easy: her father died in late 2004, and the burden of having thirteen people in her home began to tell on her aunt. But Solace has refurbished a house for her and her surviving siblings and a cousin, and funded a treatment programme for her including anti-retroviral drugs.

Ruth is a living testimony to the glory of God. It needed a move of the Spirit to bring her healing and joy. But it also needed those who ministered, counselled and prayed, and those who have provided her with a home and medicine. It is the joy of being co-workers with Christ that motivates such givers, and it is seeing the touch of God on Ruth's life which is their reward.

15

Blessed are the Peacemakers

Listen to the drums pounding mercilessly, and two gui-
tars and a keyboard struggling to overcome the tem-
peramental electrics. Watch the stage at the front of the
church, a cement-covered mud platform raised eighteen
inches off the ground. At the back some sheets of blue
and white material form a colourful backdrop. There is
a choir of fifteen or twenty young people exuberantly
praising God. As with most Rwandan evangelical
churches there are no printed words, overheads or books
– just the rhythm and passion of these African
Christians. They smile and laugh and dance as the noise,
the sweat, the movement and the dust increase.

This is the church of Paul Ndahigwa in Gatenga,
Kigali. But Paul is not only pastor of the church and vice
President of *L'Église Vivante* churches in Rwanda, he is
also leading a programme which is healing the wounds
and reconciling the hearts of Hutus and Tutsis.

'We can build roads and schools and houses, but
when the heart is full of brokenness and hatred, we will
fail again,' he explains. Paul himself was a refugee, having been taken as a young child by his fleeing parents to
Uganda to escape the killings of the early sixties. He

grew to love Jesus and began to pastor churches from his base among the refugees of the Rwandan diaspora in Uganda.

When the genocide began, the call of God came to minister to the survivors. Paul was among the first to respond to God's call. He preached in the refugee camps in partnership with David Ndaruhutse, founder of African Revival Ministries (ARM) and known as the Apostle of Africa before he was killed in a plane crash in 1997. Ndaruhutse had also set up *L'Église Vivante* in Burundi to shepherd and disciple the converts from ARM's crusades, and Paul and Ndaruhutse went on to establish the same kind of 'living church' in Rwanda.

Paul's personal battle against hatred and revenge was not won cheaply – he lost many family members; and the suffering of those who had been through the torture, rape and mutilation of the genocide made the message of forgiveness a hard one to preach. 'It was a genocide that was quite different,' explains Paul. 'We had the same culture, language and religion. Those who killed were often relatives of others who were killed. Even those who did not kill were regarded as killers if they were Hutus. And all Tutsis, whether married to a Hutu or not, were to be killed. They killed the pregnant women and ripped out the babies and they took little children and swung them against walls. Not all took part, but the accusation against those who did not was: "What did you do when others were killed? What did you do to prevent it? Did you think it was a game?"'

Every day at the camps they preached the gospel of peace. God gave Paul a message for the healing of the nation and brought him together with a facilitating ministry from Minnesota, The Pilgrim Centre for Reconciliation. They started to organise three-day retreats which brought Hutu and Tutsi together and enabled them to work through issues of hatred, bitterness, hurt and forgiveness. Those who attended studied 2 Corinthians 5:14-21 and learnt its message of unity, newness and reconciliation, then on the third day there was a time of confession. As those who participated ate and fellowshipped together, God began to work miracles. Even the pastors began to ask: 'How can we be the healers of the people until our own hearts are healed?' Thus began the vision to train facilitators of healing and reconciliation throughout Rwanda.

There are now about 250 facilitators throughout the country taking these three-day retreats, and supervising healing and reconciliation groups. There is much we can do to help the healing of Rwanda, by supporting charities like Comfort Rwanda, but the real work of healing and reconciliation has to come from the hearts of Rwandan Christians like these, who are answering the call of God to be peacemakers in the nation. In one retreat, the pastors of Ruhengeri and Umutara were brought together. Ruhengeri was a stronghold of extremism in the north-west of Rwanda and very few Tutsis survived there. *Interahamwe* infiltrators from the refugee camps in the Congo found refuge there in the years after the genocide, and the Tutsis regarded all the Hutus from Ruhengeri as 'bad people'. Many of the Ruhengeri pastors had never met a Tutsi Christian. Similarly, Umutara is the region where most of the Tutsi returnees settled, and the pastors had grown up among Tutsi exiles. Paul describes what happened: 'The pastors were surprised to see normal people from the other tribe. They began to say, "Now we can't separate; we should stay one from each tribe in the same room," and they began to make friends.'

Two particular responses sprang spontaneously from the healing and unity the pastors had discovered. They began a programme of visiting one another's churches (the programme is completely cross-denominational and breaks down denominational as well as ethnic barriers) and they began to share gifts with each other, a practice which still continues. The old suspicions have gone, replaced by a genuine respect and love.

Joseph Mugesa is one of those who has been trained to lead healing and reconciliation retreats. He has a beautiful spirit, and is the kind of man you instantly feel radiates who Jesus is. He is strongly-built with a short stubbly beard tinged with grey; his gentle sincere eyes crease into a smile, and the thick African lips soon follow. But it was not always that way: Joseph was born a refugee, and could hardly have had a worse start in life. His parents were fleeing the violence of 1962 in which many Tutsis were killed, including their own parents. They were making for the border with Uganda, but Joseph's mother was pregnant and Joseph was born while they were escaping.

After three years Joseph's family found their way to Tanzania, and he grew up enduring stigma and discrimination. He was not accepted into the Tanzanian government schools, and was educated at makeshift refugee schools. When he was seventeen Joseph became a Christian, and four years later he began to serve God full-time among the refugees and local Tanzanians. But in his heart the wound was deep, and the question was always: 'Why are we divided and refugees?' Hope arose momentarily when peace negotiations in the early 1990s raised the possibility of a return to Rwanda but when those failed and the war and genocide began, Joseph's heart was heavy. 'I witnessed the dead bodies going down the Kagera River. It refreshed my own pain and reminded me of my own beginnings. I felt helpless knowing they were cleaning out the Tutsis and I had uncles and aunts and other family there, and hatred started to build its power in my life. When the genocide finished, we entered Rwanda and found people everywhere with fresh injuries from machetes and clubs with nails.'

Joseph settled at Kibungo in the south-west and began a church with a few people. There is much poverty there, and many of the houses are made of sticks and mud with no cement to ward off the heavy downpours of the rainy season. Children chew bits of sugar cane in the absence of a proper food supply, and walk barefoot on the hot hard roads with thorns and stones.

Joseph recounts what happened when a Hutu first visited the church. 'The message I was preaching stopped because I thought he had come to kill me and finish the cleansing. He called me to speak to him but I refused. Eventually he said he had come to tell us there was a building we could meet in!'

Joseph smiles and laughs at his own fears but in those days before God had dealt with them they were very real, with good reason. 'For the next three years we had Hutus in the church but I had no love for them and I wouldn't evangelise them. I was like Jonah.' But in 1998 he found himself at a healing and reconciliation retreat. 'I didn't agree with the teaching the first time but the second time I was touched in my heart. I understood the meaning of the cross. I knew it and preached it but didn't know it could unite people with differences. I taught repentance but the thought that the cross unites people was far away.' God began to do a deep work in Joseph's heart. 'I saw Jesus receiving me and I changed my mind. I could not think there was anything good in a Hutu but now I realised there could be. The cross became very meaningful and started to heal me.'

Joseph's healing was further helped by a Hutu who stood among the people like one standing in the gap, accepting what they had done. 'He came near to me, weeping. He said that what had happened from 1959–94 was upon "us". "We destroyed your homes," he said, tears streaming down his face. "We killed your relatives, we threw them in rivers, lakes and toilets." He confessed the sins of his people like Daniel, and knelt at my feet.'

When that Hutu confessed Joseph's heart was opened, and he began to realise his own sin. 'I didn't kill them but I hated them, and that cannot allow me to be a friend of God. It was as if I was released in my heart and now I could serve God in all the tribes.'

Joseph began to get involved in the healing and reconciliation retreats. The words of Jesus, 'Come, and I will give you rest' (Mk. 6:31) were important for him, as he saw how rest could only come through repentance, forgiveness and healing. He is now a leader for the programme in the province of Kibungo. 'I know that I am healed, I am a different person. I know the truth that "I am a new creation in Christ" (2 Cor. 5:17). I used not to be able to sit beside Hutus, but now I can love them and minister to them because Jesus has set me free. I love the ministry of reconciliation.'

His eyes sparkle again and the smile breaks out. He remembers a special time at one of the retreats. 'There was a Hutu girl whose father was a *genocidaire*. He was in prison and she hated Tutsis because they made her father go to prison, but when I shared my testimony she began to wonder if it was possible that "some Tutsis might love us." God touched her heart and we had time to pray. She knelt down before me and I laid hands on her and asked God to end her sorrows and change her thinking and open her eyes to see good things in others.'

This is where the supernatural power of God takes over. God is not leaving these people to get on with sorting out their problems, he is moving supernaturally with power among them. Many who testify to wonderful healing have been helped by supernatural revelation and intervention. Joseph says: 'When I laid hands on her, she heard the Holy Spirit's voice saying, "The one who is laying hands on you is your father." She told God that this was impossible and they prayed and finished, divided into workshops, then came back and gave testimony of what God had done.'

Suddenly someone started whooping with the typical Rwandan alarm call, and giving a message from God: 'I have given somebody a father but they have neglected it. It is me that gave you that father.' Joseph was unaware of what had happened in the girl while they had been praying together and looked around with everyone else to see what was happening. Suddenly the girl, Germaine* Mukandekezi, came running and pushing through the people. 'My heart was racing,' says Joseph. 'She ran to me and embraced me and said, "You are the daddy God has given me. I heard the voice but didn't obey, but now my heart receives the message and I accept you as my father – can you accept me?" I received her and said: "I am free to be your father, be also my child." She is still my daughter and even though she is now growing up as a young adult, she often stays as my daughter.'

Germaine's father was offered clemency if he confessed and asked forgiveness, but refused to do so. When Mukandekezi told her father what God was doing in her life he said: 'You are bringing a bad thing into our family and have become a mad born-again Christian.' She is now about to be married and says: 'My father was arrested and my mother died, but God has given me a father.'

Now we are in Joseph's own church. He stands and ministers to the people in front of him. Many are survivors, but others are Hutus who see in this man of grace one who points to a Saviour of love and peace. He invites a young woman to testify. Florence* Mukamana looks young and wears a light blue top. She speaks of a remarkable change in her life.

'I was born always for sadness, but I met Jesus who removed all the sadness and sorrow.' Her church voices their agreement and encourages her to continue.

> I never saw one of my parents and the other was an animal to me. I had no one to love me and I grew up with a heart like an animal. I had great bitterness because other children are fed by their parents, but my food was to be beaten constantly. I was not allowed to call him 'Father' as he hated me. Then even he left me, and I was filled with loneliness and I had no one to comfort or protect me during the war. I was abused and raped during the genocide, and when it ended I had no one to turn to. I thought I could survive if I found a man to marry, but that was a disaster and I had to leave him. I thought God must not know me and no one on earth knows me, so I wanted to go to the forest and die so that no one would see my dead body. I preferred to be eaten by animals. I never slept, and survived by taking alcohol.
>
> Eventually I decided that I should receive Jesus, because if I die after receiving Jesus I will be happy because Jesus can take my sins away. When I went to the church they hadn't started preaching, they were praising God. I walked in and said, 'I have come to receive Jesus.' That is when I was saved, and after the service I went home and ate and smiled and slept all night. People wondered what had happened. I had never smiled; in all my life I had never smiled except under the influence of alcohol. Instead of wanting to die I know I will not die but live to testify about Jesus.

Psalm 4:7-8 asserts: 'You have put gladness in my heart, more than when their grain and new wine abound. In peace, I will both lie down and sleep, for You alone, O Lord, make me to dwell in safety.' From the moment she found Christ, Florence has slept in peace, and the need for alcohol instantly vanished. Jesus has stilled the restless fear and pain, and she is clearly delighted that she can sleep 'wonderfully' every night. For Florence the word of God has come to pass: 'You have turned for me my mourning into dancing; You have loosed my sackcloth and girded me with gladness' (Ps. 30:11). Florence is not talking about coping mechanisms and learning how to live with pain; she is talking of healing and joy. Her face is relaxed in a smile and her body is alive with expressions of eager thanks to God. 'Jesus has changed my life and now I always smile when I am with people. Before I knew Jesus I was always crying, but now I am smiling. Today as I tell you those things there is joy in my heart.'

This is what Rwanda needs thousands of times over, and this is what Joseph and his brothers and sisters in the churches in Rwanda are ministering to the broken people. It is the way the gospel is meant to affect lives, and it is doing so because it is preached with total conviction and received with total faith. There is nothing else Florence wanted except to be healed of her pain, and this is what the gospel has done. 'I was lost but now I'm living,' she declares, 'and the things I missed all my life are being restored in Jesus.'

In church, with his ministry of healing and reconciliation, Joseph is working hard and seeing God do many great things. 'The work is doing well and making progress,' he says, 'but there are many who are wounded and not yet reached. We still have a great work to reach them, but the power of the Holy Spirit will empower us and the church is the tool in God's hand.'

16

Reconciliation and the Cross

Jesus is the master at taking irreconcilable people and breaking down the walls of division through the cross; bringing peace and unity out of hatred, bitterness and division. Followers of Jesus and the church as an organisation have often lost sight of this wonderful truth in the pursuit of less important but more compelling personal agendas. 'Instead of continuing with two groups of people separated by centuries of animosity and suspicion, he created a new kind of human being, a fresh start for everybody. Christ brought us together through his death on the Cross' (*The Message* – Eph. 2:14-16). In Rwanda the animosity was only decades and not centuries old, but hatred quickly gets a hold in human hearts, and the need for reconciliation is just as great as if it had lasted for centuries.

In Christ the barriers are broken and the distinctions we make on the basis of ethnicity, culture or background are destroyed (Rom. 10:12, Col. 3:11). Both Tutsi and Hutu and any other people on the face of the earth can be born again into the body of Christ, and become one in him (1 Cor. 12:13). The response to such unity and oneness has to be a heart of compassion, kindness, humility, gentleness and patience (Col. 3:12). Jesus encouraged those who worship the Father to repair the broken and disturbed relationships around them in order to free their hearts to worship him (Mt. 5:23-24).

Once God's Word begins to break through, especially into the hearts of those who lead, preach and teach in the church, such wonderful truths are bound to produce a dramatic change in the way Christians behave to one another, and pave the way for genuine forgiveness and reconciliation. Forgiveness and reconciliation are not the same. Forgiveness is a non-optional command from God based on the sacrifice of Christ on the cross, demonstrating the extent of God's forgiveness and calling us to follow him in the same spirit of forgiving love. It is hard, but possible, to forgive without acknowledgement, repentance or change in the heart of the one we forgive.

Reconciliation, however, requires a coming together. It may be initiated by the offended party deciding to 'go and show him his fault in private' and providing the offender with an opportunity to listen, repent and be won over (Mt. 18:15, Lk. 17:3). However, even where the offended makes the first move, the offender must still listen and repent. Biblical reconciliation goes further than arbitration leading to an acceptance of a compromise; biblical reconciliation is the joining together through the cross of two people previously in opposition.

Dr David Cormack in his book *Peacing Together*[36] considers reconciliation as taking place in three stages: *disengagement, convergence and integration*. In disengagement there is an end to active hostility, in convergence the two sides come together and talk through the situation and understand each other – it is the point of contact – and the third phase of integration involves confession, repentance and forgiveness. In Rwanda reconciliation is particularly hard at this point because of the tension between the processes of justice and reconciliation.

Those in authority in Rwanda must remember the hurt of those who have lost everyone and everything, and cannot cope with those who murdered their family walking free after relatively short prison sentences. But national reconciliation is crucial in order to break the cycle of retaliation which has afflicted Rwanda for half a century. On the wall inside the genocide memorial at Gisozi, Kigali, the words of Yolande Mukagasana, a survivor of the genocide awarded the Honourable Mention for Peace Education by UNESCO in 2003, sum up this conundrum of life and death, justice and reconciliation: 'There will be no humanity without forgiveness, there will be no forgiveness without justice, but justice will be impossible without humanity.'

When the cross of Christ and the grace of God are brought into that conundrum and God's divine nature touches the weakness of man's humanity, the tension can be broken and the solution found. In fact when God breaks in there is no discernible three-stage process needed. As God changes a heart through the revelation of his own love and forgiveness, then confession, repentance and forgiveness overtake 'disengagement' and 'convergence.' The Bible calls it 'love, the perfect bond of unity' (Col. 3:14).

Biblically, confession (Jas. 5:16), repentance (2 Cor. 7:10) and forgiveness (Mt. 18:21-35) are to be given unilaterally whether other people involved respond or not. Reconciliation, however, involves the bridging of the gap between two people, and in Christ that bridge is the cross. Repentance and forgiveness are the two sides of the bridge, and reconciliation can only take place when the bridge is built right across the river. Our reconciliation to

God requires both his forgiveness through the cross and our repentance, and with two people the availability of forgiveness does not always lead to reconciliation. In forgiveness or repentance one heart needs to be changed, in reconciliation two hearts must be changed. Two people must be brought to peace.

When the work of God changes hearts and allows the peace of reconciliation to spring up, the Kingdom of God comes among his people in a striking manner and the power of the cross is demonstrated. The word of God testifies to this: 'Peacemakers who sow in peace raise a harvest of righteousness' (Jas. 3:18, NIV). In Rwanda both bridge-builders who allow their hearts to join at the cross have to work through the shocking consequences of those hundred days of murderous madness, dealing with shame and guilt on one side, and the pain and anger of loss on the other.

Although the healing of the survivor is very close to the heart of God, so also is his call for those who have sinned greatly to repent and find forgiveness. They have a great need of healing too. 'Do I have any pleasure in the death of the wicked,' declares the Lord God, 'rather than that he should turn from his ways and live?' (Ezek. 18:23). The path to healing is a hard one, but one obstacle can be removed when those who committed genocide repent and ask forgiveness. In the same way that God is working miracles among the wounded to heal them, he is working miracles among the perpetrators to bring them to repentance.

Tito Rutaremara spoke at a meeting of about six hundred widows of Solace Ministries. Over six feet tall, with his beard and hair forming a well-cropped ring of stately grey around his face, he was the parliamentary ombudsman credited with writing Rwanda's new post-genocide constitution, responsible for the integrity of the Rwandan

Parliament and highly respected in his work of maintaining its standards. He spoke to the widows with a
calm but urgent request as the hot sun baked the bare
earth and balloons put up for the special occasion burst
in the heat. Although not a believer himself he called on
the widows 'to pray for those who are still on the bad
side, because if they are not healed they will not change.'
It is obviously true but not easy to accept, as flashpoints
of conflict all over the world remind us constantly.

As I listened to him speak those words to the hundreds of women whose lives had been shattered by the
cruel violence of the killers, I wondered how they would
respond. I should have known better: they were already
praying. His words were not met with the stony silence
and penetrating stare of those who hold on to their bitterness, but with cries of *yego* (yes), and claps and promises to keep praying. Not for them the rights of the
victim to extract every last bit of justice and squeeze
the killers for every bit of guilt they can. This is where
the work of the gospel is so beautifully powerful:
instead of demanding justice for the wrongs done to
them, the widows demonstrate the grace and forgiveness that produces a sweet-smelling offering to God. It is
made possible only by the cross. When Christ has taken
the pain and sin there is no place for it on the shoulders
of his children.

Many of those caught up in the genocide have found
Christ in the prisons; some no doubt have used 'conver-
sion' as a ruse for clemency, but many have come to
Christ in genuine repentance and salvation. When those
who carried out massacres find Christ, the battle for forgiveness and cleansing is not an easy one. Nor is the task
of re-integrating former killers into society. Even if they
have repented and asked forgiveness, how should they
behave? Must they hang their heads in shame among

those whose relatives they killed, or can they be truly renewed and start life again?

The men who committed acts of genocide were not all evil monsters. Neither were the many women who were involved; in 1997, by which time a good number of the perpetrators had been arrested, over five and a half thousand women, many with dependent infants, were being held in prison (just over 5 per cent of the total prison population), most of whom had been accused of crimes of genocide. Rwandans are beautiful people, and they can't all be psychopaths. Those who killed were caught up in an ethnic ideology which they had invited into their hearts. This turned them into murderers. Some were driven by hatred, some by fear, some by ignorance. There are still many who refuse to confess or ask forgiveness, and there are others whose 'repentance' is a confession of convenience to reduce their sentence. But there are others who are miracles of the cross, proof of the power of love to change a life and rebuild a community.

17

Blessed are the Meek

The sector of Karama in the Kamonyi district of Gitarama province lies half an hour's bumpy drive off the nearest paved road. The occasional vehicle travels along the rutted, dusty red tracks, but in Karama a pair of shoes is a more likely goal to aspire to for transport. Like much of Rwanda, there is no flat land here and the mud-brick, tin-roofed houses are scattered across the slopes, surrounded by their small fields of bananas, beans and maize. Men and women are dotted around the fields, mattocks raised high in the air before they split the hard red earth and another square foot of ground is ready for planting. A few houses in close proximity form a small village, and a man sits on a shaky wooden chair selling roasted maize. A kilo of mangoes sells for the equivalent of 15 pence, if you can find a buyer.

But in Karama I witnessed a miracle, when I joined a meeting of the local healing and reconciliation group. In this small area an estimated twenty thousand Rwandans were killed. The Nyabarongo River flows through the region, and many who watched scenes of the genocide on the television news will remember the piles of bloated bodies floating down various tributaries of the Nile, including the Nyabarongo. This was an easy way of disposing of bodies, and was accompanied by a shout expressing the myth that the Tutsis come from elsewhere: 'Go back to Ethiopia where you belong!' Many of those in the Kamonyi district were thrown into the river dead or alive with this taunt in their ears. Others were killed higher up in the hills.

The building where the meeting took place is cement-coated and mud-bricked, situated at the end of a ridge which turns upwards to a eucalyptus wooded hill. When the slaughter began some of the local people came to this hill and began to defend themselves, mainly with sticks and stones. As word got out, more of those threatened with death found their way to the hill and continued the defence but the leaders of the genocide, here as elsewhere, were complicit with the government and called in the army to shoot the defenders.

Imagine this meeting: about seventy people are in the building, dimly lit through the small windows by the bright, slightly hazy sun. There are men and women in roughly equal numbers, and a mother sits suckling her baby. There are some smiles and there is a good feeling in the building, a sense of God's grace and peace. They have gathered to tell what God has done among them and are eager to tell others; they want people to understand that reconciliation is taking place, that Rwandan people are making progress, that God has done this work.

The man responsible for the healing and reconciliation groups in Gitarama, Pastor Emmanuel, begins to talk: 'We are gathered here as two ethnic groups, and we have people who were deeply involved in the genocide and confessed and asked forgiveness. There are also those who belong to a survivors' association whose families were killed by the people that are here. The survivors and doers are together because we are now one in Christ Jesus and we trust him. They are standing firm together.'

There are thirty or forty survivors and a similar number of *genocidaires* here today. Of those who survived many were abused and raped, and nine among this group contracted AIDS through rape in the genocide. Patrick Ramara* gets up to testify, announcing his intention to tell what he did in the genocide. James 5:16 tells us: 'Confess your sins to one another, and pray for one another so that you may be healed.'

'In 1994 we were determined to kill,' he begins. 'We were called by the government and appointed to do the work here.' This is not passing the buck. It is the sad but simple truth that the Rwandan government of the time was one of the strongest reasons for the success of the genocide. An ordinary man living in a mud-brick house on a hillside in the Rwandan countryside turned into a perpetrator of genocide.

Patrick points to a woman in the group who is wearing the wrap-round garment of a Rwandan woman made with a light blue patterned cloth, and an orange head-scarf. She does not react to Patrick's identification. 'We went and found the relatives of that lady where they had hidden,' he continues. 'We brought them down the hill and killed them.' We are at the foot of the hill and they were killed around here. Patrick leaves out the details, sparing the woman remembrance of the dreadful butchering of her family with machetes.

After the genocide Patrick was identified and put in prison, where preachers came and spoke the gospel to him. 'Because of what I did I wanted to receive Jesus as my Saviour, but I couldn't live with my sin.' The conviction of sin went deep into Patrick and this is no easy confession for an early release. He was determined to let the

Saviour's love reach the survivors of those he killed. He confessed to the authorities, including an admission of killing some relatives of the new government. Now that Christ has brought him into the light there is no desire to hide the truth.

Patrick's sentence was reduced but his confession and repentance did not stop there. He faced the challenge of reaching out to the survivors. 'I had to go to the woman whose family I had killed. I came and I was ashamed but when I asked forgiveness, she forgave me.' It is hard to accept the assurance of forgiveness, when you are living with those whom you have bereaved. To acknowledge the shame, and also know forgiveness, requires humility and an understanding of the cross. He speaks with simplicity and earnestness. He remembers the shame, but knows that Christ has taken it: 'We are now in this group together, and I continue talking to them and they receive me.'

Vénantie* stands up after Patrick. She is still a young woman, eleven years after the genocide. She is the woman he pointed to: her family was hacked to death by the man sitting a few rows away. Owning up to genocide is one step, but I wait tensely to see what comes from her side. Almost immediately she begins to cry; the loss of her family in such a horrific way is still painful and through the tears she talks of the big family she had. Many, many relatives were killed.

'The former government called the Hutus to kill Tutsis, but I survived as God protected me, I don't know how.' The journey from blaming God to thanking him for protection has not been an easy one. 'After the genocide, I was the head of the family. Some children survived but they all carried injuries from the wounds they received. After the war I was in a church and I started reading the Bible and came to John 3:16: "For God so loved the world that He gave His only begotten Son." I began to find some comfort in the Bible and met some people who read it, and I wanted to be with them because they comforted us. I came to realise like Job that we go through many difficulties but that God still loved us, so I read the Bible and found God is love.'

It was then that Vénantie decided to forgive. God worked in killer and survivor to bring them in his timing to this place of reconciliation. As Vénantie continues to speak the tears have gone and her voice carries the notes of hope. She has found genuine power in the love of Christ and her life bears witness to it. Forgiveness at an ethnic level ('I forgive the Hutus') is not the same as forgiveness at a personal level. Although many survivors recognise the need for reconciliation in order to build a new Rwanda, there are far fewer who will reach out to those who bear the personal responsibility for killing their family. Only such reconciliation allows survivor and perpetrator to truly relate. There are many, including Christians, who are not yet able to go this far, and others who have offered forgiveness which has not been met with repentance. Reconciliation takes extraordinary courage on both sides: the perpetrators are shamed by the enormity of what they have done, and many of the survivors have no desire to see them, let alone forgive them.

Vénantie is an exceptional woman. She talks of how God protected Patrick from dying in prison, where overcrowding killed many. I struggle to comprehend her grace towards her family's killer. She wants the world to know the power of the cross to bring healing and reconciliation, and her forgiveness towards Patrick is an extravagant overflow. 'I want to show that I forgive,' she says. She walks over to him, they embrace with the strong hug of true friends and Vénantie smiles. This is the power of the cross, described in Ephesians 2:16: 'The Cross got us to embrace, and that was an end of the hostility' (*The Message*).

The President of a widows' organisation, in a speech the previous week, pleaded for the church to do what seemed impossible: change the hearts of *genocidaires*. He was angry at the continued refusal of killers and their accomplices to repent, and at the church for not standing against the genocide. Had he been here, surely hope would have touched his heart.

André is another *genocidaire*. He killed the sister of the man, Daniel, sitting next to me. As I look at him, I also notice a musty, unpleasant smell which seems to be growing in the room. André also killed two sons of Beata, another woman here. This is a room of killers and survivors, and André was a leader of the killers. 'I was in the former government when we were instructed to kill, and I was leading others to kill.' Such serial murder is the product of a dehumanising ideology: a hardened heart and a poisoned mind can become terrible tools in the hands of the devil. André was captured and imprisoned after the genocide, and he heard the word of God in prison. 'When I received the word of God,' he said, 'I realised what I had done, so I decided to repent and ask forgiveness.' The Bible says we are 'born again of the living and imperishable word' (1 Pet. 1:23). What incredible power there is when Spirit and Word combine to change a life like André's!

He confessed and received early release. Many survivors complain bitterly that this favours perpetrators over survivors, an understandable grudge: but when former killers like André humble themselves before the relatives of their victims, God starts to work in the survivors. The instrument of pain becomes a channel of healing. André explains: 'As we were allowed to re-integrate we decided to go, bearing our shame, and ask forgiveness. They decided to forgive and make this group. We want to tell the truth of what took place. We want to show people we were very bad in '94 but we are no longer the same. We used to fear the victims' families because we were guilty, but when we formed the group we are one.' This is church as it should be, making two groups into one, proving the power of the cross to remove the walls of hostility and hatred. Of the seventy people in the room, most cannot afford the three thousand Rwandan francs (£3) it takes to buy a Bible, but they are learning how to live out its message.

Daniel rises from the wooden bench we are sitting on. I lean back, not realising there is a door behind me, and almost fall backwards off the bench as it begins to open. The smell seems to intensify, and Daniel catches me and closes the door.

He has an intelligent look and talks with a forceful but gentle earnestness. He also chides the former government who 'wanted us to kill each other', and his bewilderment at such a policy is clear. 'We had intermarried, we were giving each other cows as a sign of friendship, we were each others' godparents.' He explains how he hid from the killers and managed to survive, and adds: 'I was actually hunted very much.' For those who were unable to escape over the border into Burundi, Congo, Tanzania or RPF-held territory, it was hard to avoid the killers. They roamed the area looking for survivors, they had lists of Tutsis and they killed systematically, ticking off the names one by one. Many who didn't kill were sympathisers, or too scared not to reveal the Tutsis being sought. Many survivors talk of how previously friendly neighbours suddenly became enemies.

Daniel ascribes his survival to 'the hand of God protecting me'. Loving André as his brother in Christ, he wants to emphasise the reality of forgiveness. He touches his bosom and speaks with conviction: 'I forgive him from the bottom of my heart.' It makes me think that what we call forgiveness doesn't penetrate far into our hearts.

Daniel walks over to the man who killed his family, and embraces him as a friend. I sense the sweet aroma of God's grace: but there is another smell still troubling me.

18

Restitution and Forgiveness

The healing and reconciliation meeting is still going on at Karama. The room is dark and hot with an unpleasant smell, but I drink in the miracle unfolding before me. Stephen* is speaking. Like the other two men he is still young, and would have been very young at the time of the genocide. In April '94 he was on the village council, working with the government to kill local Tutsis. He points to Marguerite:* 'We went to her home and killed more than four people.' Marguerite elaborates: 'He killed five.'

Like Patrick and André, Stephen was imprisoned as a killer. That was where he heard the gospel. 'They came and taught us the word of repentance and to ask forgiveness. It entered my life and I decided to go and ask forgiveness.' These Rwandans understand the gospel! Marguerite explains: 'When he was in the prison he wrote asking for forgiveness, but I wanted him to die.' But while God was dealing with Stephen in prison, his testimony to Marguerite began to bear fruit. She started reading the Bible. 'I came to realise God wants me to forgive the sinner.' When Stephen was released he went to find Marguerite to seek forgiveness, and found her trying to build a home. He was the one who had destroyed her house in the genocide after killing her family. Although she recognised the need to forgive, Marguerite was still struggling to accept Stephen's repentance, but he started making bricks to help her rebuild her home. The ex-prisoners emphasise repeatedly that they have strong arms, and will use their strength to help the survivors whom they bereaved. They have little money, but they will prove their repentance with deeds of care. Although the government takes the blame for the ideology of genocide, these men take personal responsibility for their sin and they back up their testimony with action. Stephen's love finally won Marguerite over: 'I had a feeling he had made a true confession.'

Those who confessed had to appear before the local courts called *Gacaca*, meaning 'justice on the grass'. These traditional local courts have been adapted for the massive task of judging tens of thousands of genocide suspects, still untried after years in jail. The first *Gacaca* sat on 10 March 2005. Defendants must reveal all the details of their own and others' part in the genocide. Village elders in Rwanda are known as *inyangamugayo* or 'men of integrity', and each *Gacaca* has nine 'judge *inyangamugayo*' and five deputies elected by the local population.[37] They undergo intensive training and at least a hundred people must be present for the *Gacaca* to sit. Different categories have been developed to deal with the different levels of suspects' involvement in the genocide:[38]

Category 1:

- Persons whose criminal acts or whose acts of criminal participation place them among the organisers, instigators, supervisors, and leaders of the crime of Genocide or of a crime against humanity;

- Persons who acted in positions of authority at the National, Provincial, District, Sector or Cell level, or in a political party, the army, religious organisations or in a militia and who perpetrated or fostered such crimes;
- Notorious murderers who by virtue of the zeal or excessive malice with which they committed atrocities, distinguished themselves in their areas of residence or where they passed;
- Persons who committed acts of sexual torture or violence.

Category 2:

Persons whose criminal acts or whose acts of criminal participation place them among the perpetrators, conspirators or accomplices of intentional homicide or of serious assault against the person – causing death.

Category 3:

Persons whose criminal acts or whose acts of criminal participation make them guilty of other serious assaults against the person.

Category 4:

Persons who committed offences against property.

Rwanda was divided into twelve Provinces (changed to five at the start of 2006) roughly the size of a small-to-medium

British county, each with an average population of six hundred thousand, though increasing year on year. These were divided into between six and fourteen Districts which in turn were divided into ten to twenty Sectors of around ten thousand inhabitants, and then local Cells with several hundred people in each. The *Gacaca* of the Cells can hear and try category 4 cases, those of the Sector can hear and try category 3, District *Gacaca* have the power to try category 2 suspects, and the Provinces deal with appeals from the lower courts. With about nine thousand Cells in the country, the organisation involved and the numbers participating have made this a massive exercise. The consequences of being found guilty at the *Gacaca* depend on the crime and the response of the perpetrator, and can range from paying reparation where property was destroyed to thirty years' imprisonment where life was taken. The process is far from simple, and demands imposed on those who have confessed are not always acceptable to those who have been bereaved. Rwandan President Paul Kagame recognises that more is expected of the survivors than the perpetrators: '. . . the survivors . . . bear almost the full burden of reconciliation. The others . . . or those associated with them, or those who didn't care what happened – are doing less . . . to remedy the situation. The burden is always put on the shoulders of the survivors, but that's also the cost of the reconciliation and the rebuilding process we have to be involved in for a better future for all of us. So we shall always feel indebted to the survivors.'[39]

In addition, for those who have not yet faced the pain, having the details of how their loved ones were killed revealed to them for the first time through a public disclosure can be extremely distressing. Some *Gacaca*, in places where there were few survivors and many were involved in the killing, struggle to find enough people of integrity who are not implicated themselves; and over twenty-seven thousand *inyangamugayo* out of the one hundred and seventy thousand elected have been dropped from the *Gacaca* after being implicated themselves. There are also regular murders of people about to testify in *Gacaca*, including Nyirabera Consolee from one of the fellowship groups run by Solace Ministries in Nyanza. She was poisoned to stop her testifying in 2004, just after being put on anti-retroviral drugs which had started to dramatically improve her health since she contracted HIV/AIDS through rape in the genocide.

The stated purposes of the *Gacaca* include putting an end to the culture of impunity for racial crimes, demonstrating the ability of local communities to solve their own problems, reviving traditional forms of dispensing justice, moving people towards reconciliation, speeding up the trial process, and revealing the truth. Such aims are in many cases being met, and most Rwandans support these courts.

When Stephen came before the *Gacaca*, Marguerite was ready to testify about her forgiveness. 'She continued saying "I forgive him" before the judges,' Stephen says appreciatively. Marguerite agrees: 'In front of the *Gacaca* I also said "I forgive this man."' So Stephen's early release was confirmed, but the work of rebuilding their lives goes on. In this community, almost twelve years after the genocide, remains are still being located and gathered for burial. When the meeting finishes, Daniel opens the door behind us and there is a fresh blast of the unpleasant smell as a pile of human remains is revealed lying on the floor. These are the latest that have been recovered. The sites are often identified many years later, and the remains of those killed given a decent burial. Such burials are always conducted with great respect and dignity – moving and painful, but conferring true dignity on the deceased and the survivors.

Alexis Ahorushakiye is the leader of a survivors' group, and explains how important this is: 'The . . . reason we love the group is that there are brethren who had relatives killed who didn't know where they were thrown, but those who confess and repent help to find them. We are glad that we are now going to bury them as real people, as it helps survivors when they can bury their loved ones.'

Up on the hill a hundred metres away they have dug a huge vault, to house the remains of those they have found and to provide a memorial, like many memorials where thousands and tens of thousands are laid to rest, the one here will hold eight of the twenty thousand killed here. Coffin upon coffin fills the vault, each holding the remains of many victims, and those in the room behind me will be laid to rest next. Such fresh reminders of the genocide form a background to the rebuilding of lives. Karama has found new hope in the cross, and Stephen talks of how he and Marguerite help each other: 'We are together now in Christ, and when she has a need she calls me and we help one another more than normal people.' Marguerite says of her new relationship with Stephen: 'I continue to pray for him that God would help us to continue living in peace and helping each other.'

Out on the hillsides is the evidence of this help, where the ex-prisoners in this group have built homes for the survivors. They use their own hands to make the bricks or erect the wooden branch framework to be filled with mud, and then 'pray in' the tin roofing. So far God has supplied their needs through various donors and the newest house being built is for Seraphine,* an orphan. She has survived with just one younger brother, and was seven when the genocide wiped out the rest of her family and relatives. Taking shelter wherever she could find a temporary willing host, she has gone from house to house for eleven years. Now she stands in front of her house, which is under construction and measures about twelve by fifteen feet. It will be a labour of love and very welcome. The thick branches stand upright in the trenches, ready to be interlaced with smaller branches and packed with mud. Marked off by trenches are two bedrooms, each the size of a single bed. An actual bed would be a bonus. But Seraphine smiles at the outcome of love: a home at long last, a place for her and her brother to call their own.

Alexis has a certificate of training for his leadership of the group that he cherishes. It has written on it: 'Now all these things are from God, who reconciled us to Himself through Christ and gave us the ministry of reconciliation. Therefore, we are ambassadors for Christ, as though God were making an appeal through us; we beg you on behalf of Christ, be reconciled to God' (2 Cor. 5:18,20). He lost all his family and relatives in the massacres but came to Christ after the genocide, and his greatest desire is to serve God: 'I came to realise that we who are still living had to understand if we continued the way we were we would perish.' He understood that the prisoner is not only the person in jail, but the man or woman who is imprisoned by bitterness.

Alexis was among the first to release his burden and begin to forgive those who killed his family. 'Pastor Emmanuel helped me until the bitterness left my heart, and so our ministry began – to train others and carry on the work of healing and reconciliation. We decided to do it voluntarily, so I visited the prisons and preached the gospel. When prisoners were released they were familiar with repentance and forgiveness, and wanted to meet survivors and ask for forgiveness. We used prayer and the word of God, and handed our burdens over to God.'

Alexis also speaks of the rebuilding programme: 'We build shelters for widows and orphans with no homes. Those who are released have no wealth and neither did the survivors, as things were destroyed. But they had arms and strength so we gathered our strength and built shelters.' He emphasises how important this is in the process of reconciliation: 'If you forgive but still have nowhere to stay and have to wander to find shelter, you can start to feel bitter again.' Alexis asks for prayer: for ex-prisoners and survivors to be integrated into the life of the community, for those who have no Bibles, and for those who are HIV positive – in this remote area it is difficult to get help to them. Looking forward to the future he seeks prayer for healing retreats, so that more Rwandans can find Christ and be healed. And he seeks prayer for new roofs for the houses, and cattle and goats for the widows and orphans. But most of all he asks that 'you always remember us so that we hand our issues over to the Lord.'

19

Signs of Hope and Healing

The sector of Mugina lies at the end of a long, red dirt road twenty kilometres to the south-west of Kigali, but double that by the circuitous tracks winding round the hills. It suffered one of the many large massacres of the genocide, and bears the scars. Today, however, is a good day for the bereaved women of Mugina: they are about to receive 42 goats, the first batch of two hundred which will be given to the widows' association here. There are more than two hundred widows in the association, and two hundred and fifty orphans who have lost families, relatives, friends, homes and livelihoods. They are the survivors from a community that lost thirty thousand people in a day.

These survivors are meeting together. They gather under the spreading branches of a leafy tree which provides a large circle of shade from the noonday sun. Thirty metres away is a hexagonal brick building containing large coffins packed with the bones of the men, women and children who were hemmed into the compound here and killed. A book of remembrance is open on a wooden podium surrounded by flowers, quickly withered in the tropical heat. Gakiga* looks after the building and its remains. The back of his head has a long, deep indent where a machete came crashing down, there are two five-inch wounds on the side of his head and a large scar streaks across his right cheek. The top half of his nose flaps over the bottom half, separated by another slash of the machete, a large red scar covers most of the back of his left hand which is fixed at right angles to his wrist, and long scars mark his legs at various points where his tendons and muscles were slashed to stop him escaping.

Gakiga was part of the huge crowd crammed into the church compound that was surrounded and weakened after days of being held captive by the encircling *interahamwe*. When they were weak enough the killers attacked with machetes, spears and clubs. They killed the men, women and children without mercy, not sparing anyone. When the fatigue of hours of killing forced them to stop slashing and hacking, they forced the remaining helpless remnant down to the river and threw them in to drown. Gakiga lay with his open wounds among the bodies for a week before being found, clinging to life, by Red Cross workers. He is eager to join the widows today to celebrate the gift of the goats.

The widows begin to sing and worship, their rhythmic voices and bodies quickly establishing the tune. An elderly widow wearing an orange, yellow, green and black wrap-round begins to dance with arms outstretched and palms lifted to God. Others join in and they sing songs of praise, then testify to God's goodness. 'It all starts with God and it finishes with God,' their leader says simply. She reads from his word: 'He who dwells in the shelter of the Most High will abide in the shadow of the Almighty. I will say to the Lord, "My refuge and my fortress, My God in whom I trust!"' (Ps. 91:1-2). Their gathering under the spreading shady branches mirrors their spiritual sheltering under the out-stretched arms of God.

The group began with three widows seeking help, and has grown quickly to the 450 widows and orphans who now work together. They meet once a month to comfort and encourage each other, and to solve such problems as funding school materials and sheltering the homeless. As with all such groups, the restoration of lives shattered in the genocide is a complex process. As the widows sing and worship, the sound of hammers on a vault being built to house the freshly collected remains of those who died mixes with the bleating of goats waiting their turn to be distributed. The needs for emotional recovery, spir-itual restoration, physical provision and the repair of a person's ability to build relationships are all part of the mosaic of healing. It is not just hearts but houses that were destroyed, not just fathers that were taken away but faith and hope as well. Even if the heart is healed and faith restored, it is hard for survivors to maintain a con-sistent standard of food, health and education provision.

God has always urged his people to provide for the bereaved. The widows and orphans of Israel were to share in eating the tithe with the Levites (Deut. 14:29), and their needs were frequently brought to the attention of God's people. As the book of James succinctly puts it: 'If a brother or sister is without clothing and in need of daily food, and one of you says to them, "Go in peace, be warmed and filled", and yet you do not give them what is necessary for their body, what use is that?' (Jas. 2:15-16). One of the first criticisms of the early church was their failure to serve food daily for the widows (Acts 6:1).

Furthermore, the healing of bitterness and unforgive-ness is made considerably easier if the survivor is not reminded daily of the consequences of their ordeal. Many survivors lost homes and possessions as well as their husbands' income, and help to replace these necessities – even a bed – can assist their recovery.

The pattern of support developed amongst these widows' associations demonstrates how God can use his people to tackle complex needs. The starting point is the broken soul. The burden carried for many years is hidden. It lies there, sometimes revealed in the sunken eyes and faraway stare that join the past and the future in one seamless stretch of hopelessness. And when there is a heart of compassion and a genuine interest in the sufferer's pain, then the boil of the soul is lanced.

Some survivors have hidden the truth for fear of being judged by friends, relatives or family. Many are guilt-ridden just because they survived and others died. Others are afraid people will think they compromised with the killers. Those who have been raped, especially those with HIV/AIDS, are concerned they will be rejected because of what has happened to them. For many, releasing their hidden burden and being met with indifference is a costly risk.

These deep secrets make a heavy load, and the priority for supporters is to help the hurting person become open to the truth. Guilt and fear start to be broken when truth is spoken, and breaking guilt and fear enables God's healing to begin. Most of those who listen to the survivors have themselves suffered much. They believe God has specifically commanded them to comfort the widows and orphans, and they can listen with real empathy and compassion. Although there is little professional trauma counselling in Rwanda, some experts advocate lay counselling as a more effective way of helping people move forward. Psychotherapist Robert

Carkhuff[40] has found that lay people with high levels of empathy, respect and self-disclosure produced the biggest positive changes in those receiving counselling. They cared so much about them, and poured themselves so deeply into helping, that those who received the help responded well.

The testimony of widows and orphans confirms this: the ability of their counsellors to enter into their sufferings with them started a process of healing. God has composed the human body and the church body to respond to consolation, fellowship, tender affection and compassion (Phil. 2:1). His comfort is designed to be passed on (2 Cor. 1:4, 7:6-7), and the burdens of those who suffer and weep should be shared and carried by those who are strong (Rom. 12:15; Gal. 6:2). He sends his servants to bind up the broken-hearted under the anointing of his Spirit. 'Death and life are in the power of the tongue' (Prov. 18:21), and the wise and compassionate counselling given by servants of God in Rwanda is helping many to rebuild a full life.

However, healing is not in wise counsel itself, but in Christ. The compassion and wisdom in the counselling enables the survivors to open their heart to the real source of healing. On the cross Christ 'bore our grief', 'carried our sorrows' and was 'scourged for our healing' (Is. 53:4-5). His shame, his pain, his humiliation, his nakedness, were a direct exchange for ours: not only was our sin borne on his shoulders, but also our pain, our humiliation and our desperate aloneness. This is the core message that is ministered to the widows and orphans, along with the wonderful blessing that he is a husband to the widow (Is. 54:4-5) and a father to the orphan (Ps. 68:5).

Becoming involved in fellowship is a further step in repairing the brokenness. Fellowship is a crucial part of the healing process, as the sense of betrayal and subsequent isolation are very strong among survivors. Many survivors and their families who were killed were betrayed by neighbours, friends, relatives, employers or employees, and no one helped or intervened for fear of being branded a sympathiser. The world stood by and watched. Friends and family they would have turned to after the genocide had been killed, and the stigma of rape and AIDS has kept them quiet about the pain and shame they carried. It was a lonely, desperate fight and many widows and orphans feel that no one can share what they have experienced, that their ordeal was different from everyone else's. And in a way it is, because 'the heart knows its own bitterness' (Prov. 14:10). It is common among survivors to avoid meeting people, to stay in their homes and trust no one, and over time they become unable to make relationships. Fellowship with others who have found healing and peace in Christ enable the lonely fight to become a shared journey of hope.

Many of the orphans refer to Jean Gakwandi and Ben Kayumba who comfort and counsel them as 'papa', and the widows (and occasionally widowers) see each other as brothers and sisters in God's family. It is a real experience of family and not a theological nicety. Josette Mukamana,* who had her husband, five children and almost all her other relatives killed, and survived a brutal rape, describes this reality: 'I praise God for bringing me to Solace Ministries. I know that I've got a family and new friends who love me. My tears change to joy because I am not alone.' Her words are repeated by many others.

There are two activities that provide the framework for the fellowship associations: the first is to pray together, and the second is small-scale income generation projects.

Survivors are encouraged to find other widows and
orphans in their area and to pray in their homes, as well
as coming to meetings for prayer, testimony, praise and
worship. Some widows and orphans will rise at 3.00 a.m.
to walk for six hours to reach these meetings. For those
who have hidden their pain for many years the prayer
meeting can be an eye-opener: they see that those who
have lost husbands and children and been raped and
infected with HIV/AIDS can dance before God, and
thank him for the new family God has given them. This
gives them hope for their own future, and the presence of
God here strengthens them.

For rape survivors or HIV/AIDS victims, fellowshipping with others who have not been affected is important in counteracting their loneliness and shame. Mutual
acceptance is a powerful aid to restoring a widow's
appreciation of herself as created in the image of God. To
know that they are fearfully and wonderfully made and
known by God is easier when there are others who tell
them so.

Josette has learned embroidery and crochet in an association in Kigali, and found the fellowship there deeply
moving. For seven years she lived a lonely and broken
life, unable even to look in a mirror and comb her hair or
wear decent clothes, distraught and hopeless with pain:
'I hated God, hated the church, hated everybody and
couldn't be with people.' She has reaped the benefits of
genuine fellowship and now her thick frizzy hair is carefully tended and she wears a lively yellow, green and
orange dress. Tears fall down her smooth soft skin as she
describes how her hatred has melted: 'I love people
now, and since I believed in Jesus Christ, my hope is in
him and everything is possible and the future is his.'

Prayer is more than just fellowship, and there are evil
forces that need to be broken among the survivors. Paul

reminds us that the real battle is against spiritual powers that war against God's people, and that part of the armour of God is prayer: 'With all prayer and petition pray at all times in the Spirit' (Eph. 6:12). The survivors learn to pray with power and accompany their prayer with fasting and overnight prayer, and as they wait on God they are strengthened.

Denise, one of the counsellors, explains her approach: 'We encourage the widows to pray to God and fast. God is our Creator and he has an answer for everything, therefore nothing is impossible before God.' Such active reliance on God helps the survivors to connect with immeasurable resources for healing and wholeness. It was Augustine who said: 'Christ is the complete physician of our wounds'[41] and the truth of that is borne out as those who seek him with all their hearts find deep peace and inner healing.

20

Widows Working Together

Even a small income can make a huge difference to a widow, an orphan or a child-headed household. Despite a rapidly increasing urban population in Kigali, the large majority of Rwandans farm a small plot with potatoes ('Irish' and sweet), beans, tomatoes, maize, cassava, sorghum, bananas and various other crops that earn the growers on average less than 60 pence a day. Many have no spare crops for cash sale, and live from harvest to harvest on what the poor soil can produce. In the city there are few fields, and no harvest means no food. So income-generating projects are essential for helping widows and orphans out of the poverty cycle. These include mushroom growing, dairy cattle, vegetable farming, goat rearing, cash crop growing (pineapples, groundnuts), bee keeping, pig rearing, soap making, tailoring, bakery products, hairdressing and craft-making.

Vineranda was one of the first to find her way to the widows' association that Solace Ministries set up in 1995, and she is adamant that prayer and listening to the word of God are the most helpful aids to her recovery. But her weight continued to fall because of poverty, and when she got involved in a bakery project and embroidery work her weight increased from less than six and a half stone (40 kgs.) to just over eleven (70 kgs.). Whether or not the bakery was especially instrumental in that, she didn't say! Margaret Uwimabera is also grateful for the help of an income-generation project. Left as a widow to look after six children, she has learnt how to bake and sell tasty African doughnuts and can now buy previously unobtainable clothes, school materials and regular food for the children.

Rural Rwanda, like much of Africa, suffers problems of impoverished soil and unpredictable harvests. A goat can improve this situation considerably. Its manure is highly prized, and can boost crop production by five hundred per cent (though thirty to fifty per cent is more usual), whilst water retention and soil pH are also improved.[42] Goats also provide milk, and a female can produce three kids a year for sale at a price equivalent to a labourer's wages for a month, so it is easy to see why widows whoop and dance and sing when they receive their goats.

Many Rwandan families and communities lost their entire cattle stock in the genocide. The milk that cattle produce is highly prized: it is an important addition to a diet often restricted to beans, bananas and vegetables. Having a cow means you have your own milk – a sign of well-being, and an opportunity for cash income. Cow manure is an even better fertiliser than that of the goats, and calves are highly valued.

Cattle in Rwandan culture occupy an important place. Their arrival at a wedding as a dowry can lead to long discussions between the two families about the respective merits of the cows and the bride, the bridegroom meanwhile being forgotten! Cattle were traditionally herded by Tutsis, and were slaughtered during the genocide out of spite. Solace Ministries has started supplying widows' groups with good quality cattle. Renewing the herds helps the whole community: when a widows' association receives cattle they become the common property of the group. The milk is sold and the money distributed to meet the greatest need. Calves can also be passed on to other widows' groups to lift them out of the poverty trap. Groups which have received cattle report a new sense of self-worth and community, as the herd provides a focus for working and fellowshipping together.

Fellowship among the widows draws the whole community in to what God is doing. As isolation, loneliness, mistrust, hatred and fear are broken down among one group, others are encouraged to move from being onlookers to participants. At one of the groups in Nyanza, towards the south of Rwanda, a widows' group have been given cows. The local dignitaries, widows and various guests made their speeches, then a cowherd eulogised and named each cow in turn. Yet the most significant aspect of the gathering was the first coming together of Tutsi, Hutu and Twa in a joint celebration. Barriers were broken down, relationships built and prejudices left behind. Many other widows' fellowship groups have brought together those separated by the genocide.

The widows and orphans are not graspers: they do not take with both hands, but receive graciously with one hand and give back from their meagre resources with the other. Money is shared between members of the group. Muteteli Donata's group makes postcards with banana leaves which they have started exporting to Germany and the UK. There are now sixty-four in the group, and she explains: 'We can now buy school materials, books and shoes.'

There is a strong commitment among all the groups to help those who have the greatest needs. Some of the income-generating groups tithe their income for poorer widows and orphans in other areas. Many give their time for nothing to train others. This is important to improve the quality of goods such as baskets, cards, jewellery, toy animals and crocheted handbags which are now being sold in small quantities to Europe and the USA. Beata, one of the trainers, says she can earn ninety pounds in a very good month from her embroidery and crocheting. That is the kind of wage that can free a person from a cycle of poverty, school their children, and pay for basic health care. If widows and orphans can obtain food, education and health, then the poverty cycle is broken.

The fellowship groups involve the beneficiaries in all the decision-making. Whether the concern is education, home-based care for disabled and sick members, or housing needs, the fellowship group is there to help. They also provide support with funeral costs and help in exhuming the remains of loved ones from pit latrines or mass graves.

Exhumation is painful for surviving family members as remains usually still bear hair, clothes and visible features which severely shock those retrieving them. Recently one of the heads of a child-headed household, Gilbert, had twenty-seven family members located. The sight of his family's bodies, the stench of the exhumation, and the trauma of the process left him distressed for several weeks until further counselling brought him back to peace. Such after-shock is common, but it is widely agreed that the process of locating, exhuming and re-burying remains should continue. After help is given to work through the re-traumatisation, there is relief for survivors who can at last bury their loved ones.

The care of those with HIV/AIDS also involves the distribution of anti-retroviral (ARV) drugs. Since the start of 2004, when only two thousand of the country's estimated quarter to half a million people living with HIV/AIDS were receiving ARV drugs (many paying the cost themselves), the number of patients receiving ARV treatment has significantly increased.[43] A National HIV/AIDS Strategic Plan, an HIV/AIDS Treatment and Care Plan, and a National Prevention Plan have all been introduced, but the number of people needing urgent help massively outstrips the available resources. At around £35 a month for treatment, most Rwandans would need two months' wages to pay for one month's drugs.

With overseas help (including funds from the UK Department for International Development channelled via the survivors' fund, SURF) Solace has begun its own ARV treatment programme which is playing its part in restoring the lives of those with AIDS. Some widows who were confined to bed, awaiting death, are now actively farming their land and looking forward to the future.

Once widows and orphans have experienced God's restoring power in their lives, they are full of thanks and want to share the message of hope with others. A 'discipleship team' of widows and orphans who have been comforted reaches out across the country to those who are still suffering. They share what they have experienced, and look to God for healing.

In addition to the discipleship team the widows have created an 'encouragement team' whose members visit and support others in difficulty, whether through poverty, illness or HIV/AIDS. They visit and provide for hospital patients, help mothers with many children, and pray with those who are sick. Evaste Mukacyubahiro was widowed and left with two children and two other dependants while handicapped, severely depressed and without an income. 'When I saw people coming to visit me it gave me hope and encouraged me to work,' she recalls, smiling broadly. 'When they comforted me I received hope, and when they showed me love I began to reach out to others.'

The youth have also created an encouragement team to visit other orphans at school and support their education, urging them to work hard and be a good example as children of God. There is a high proportion of boarding schools in the Rwandan education system. Parents can visit their children once a month, but orphans have no one to visit them. For widows and orphans, the provision of 'family' is fundamental, making a huge difference to those who have lost relatives. In the words of one orphan girl: 'I was sick at school, but when I saw the youth from Solace who visited me I became healthy.'

What difference does the restoration of family make to the widows and orphans? It's the difference between light and darkness, life and death. Denise, one of the counsellors, puts this in her own words: 'The plan of the devil was to kill us or make us beggars, but the plan of God is to make us alive and to work for our bright future. We will not die, but we will live to tell to people in all the nations how God is faithful and powerful.'

Motivated by Tragedy

In south-west Rwanda the poverty is tangible, and the acidic soil makes the daily battle to grow food doubly hard. The car stops beside a small rough cross at the side of the road and the man beside me in the driver's seat gets out and walks across the road. A gaggle of children is running about in dirty, torn T-shirts and bare feet. A few banana trees are dotted around and a couple of houses, the walls coloured by the deep, red-brown Rwandan mud that is their main building material. Half a dozen women are waiting to greet the traveller, head-scarves protecting them from the high noon sun, their old T-shirts contrasting with the bright but faded colours of their wrap-round skirts. The man embraces them, and they smile and welcome him gladly. This is Jean Gakwandi's home village. The cross marks the grave of his father, mother, sister, brother, cousin, aunt and grandmother. The women he embraces are the 'prison widows' of the men, now in jail, who killed his family. It is remarkable evidence of forgiveness and grace, but Jean is a remarkable man.

The work of Solace is inspired by its director, Jean Gakwandi, and is the fulfilment of a promise he made to

God that, should he live through the genocide, he would dedicate the rest of his life to helping the survivors. He is filled with a vision for the healing of those widows and orphans, and convinced of the power of the gospel to realise that vision. This man, so familiar with the shattered lives of thousands, says: 'The tragedy of 1994 has shown us that we believe in a living and loving God.'

Jean grew up in the shadow of racial hatred, his childhood marred by having his relatives killed, his home burnt down, his belongings looted and his family's cattle taken, slaughtered and eaten. Forty years on he still remembers the nights they spent sleeping in the open as his father desperately sought to replace their ruined home. Some of his relatives fled to Congo, but in Rwanda the persecution increased and at Christmas 1963 there was another spate of violence and Jean first saw people being killed. Many of his schoolteachers were murdered and his friends orphaned; and although his own parents survived, his aunt Julienne and some relatives were burnt to death in their home. Unknown to Jean, Viviane, the woman he would later marry, was orphaned at the same time.

While Jean was training to be a doctor, the persecution took a new twist. In 1973 a fresh wave of killings swept the country, Jean was put on a list of unwanted citizens, and his name was hung on public noticeboards. One day, while assisting in an operation, he was told to remove his gloves and leave his job. He had been born again three years before and had recently been baptised in the Holy Spirit. It stood him in good stead, enabling him to avoid resentment and stay strong in his faith. On one occasion, when a military car approached and a young girl pulled him into a sorghum plantation to hide, God assured him of protection, and from that time on Jean knew his life was in God's hands. He was being taught how to trust God in danger and it was a lesson that would be seriously tested, but always trusted, many years later.

Twenty years on it is the night of 6 April 1994. Kigali is waiting in fear for the unleashing of terror after the President's plane has been shot down. God is speaking to Jean and his family through their evening reading. It is Proverbs 18:10 – *Izina ry'Uwiteka ni umunara ukomeye, umukiranutsi awuhungiramo, agakomera*: 'The name of the Lord is a strong tower, the righteous runs into it and is safe.' The other verses are equally emphatic, from Deuteronomy 33:26-27: 'There is none like the God of Jeshurun, who rides the heavens to your help, and through the skies in his majesty. The eternal God is a dwelling place, and underneath are the everlasting arms; and he drove out the enemy from before you and said "Destroy!"'

It is early morning on 7 April, and the noise of screaming has punctuated the night as neighbours and friends are slaughtered. As dawn breaks at 6.00 a.m., the screams continuing, Presidential Guards arrive at Jean's house. Like a number of the better-built houses in the city, it has a wall and locked gates round the house and garden, and iron bars on the glass windows. As soon as they hear the Presidential Guards, Jean is prompted by God to go with his wife Viviane and their four children and the housegirl, to hide in a small store-room and pray that God will confuse and blind the attackers. The killers shoot open the locks on the gates and fire their guns through every window, carpeting the house with broken glass, but fail to see any sign of the family and leave. After their escape the family are left shaken, wondering at the folly of ethnic hatred.

The memories, though healed, are still vivid in Jean's mind. The family stay almost motionless, not eating or drinking for 37 hours in the store-room, unsure who is still around. All they can do is pull the telephone into the room and whisper down the line to friends and relatives. Viviane speaks to some good friends who have been robbed by Presidential Guards but escaped. She warns them the killers will come back but there is little they can do, and by the afternoon they are dead. Other friends abroad are contacted, and a prayer-chain springs into action.

Two days later, God prompts Jean and the family to pray intensely. During the night Viviane has had a vision of an army of angels protecting them and they pray hard, trusting that God is watching over them. Fifteen minutes later the *interahamwe* return and start to shoot through the windows, at wardrobes and beds and anywhere anyone could be hiding. The family's hearts are pounding as they hear the killers climbing up to the store-room window. By now they know that many people have been killed by grenades thrown through windows, and Viviane asks the children if they are ready before God to die. Jean is still convinced God will protect them, and the killers leave without throwing any grenades.

Jean has guessed by now that the killers are phoning Tutsi homes where they suspect people are still alive, and they stop answering calls. In the meantime a friend has convinced the Swiss ambassador, Marie France, to try to rescue the family. Bravely she agrees, and as she approaches their street a group of killers tries to follow her but are thwarted because they run out of petrol. The family and the housegirl pile into the car and drive off. Once more they pray that God will blind and confuse the killers, and surely God does so as they drive straight through a roadblock of Presidential Guards. Marie France takes them to friends who work for the 'Swiss

Co-operation' and are prepared to risk their lives to shelter them. Jean and his family will hide there for 89 days. By the end of the first day there are 21 people in the home, 17 of them in hiding.

Two days later, their hosts Wolfgang and Marianne and their two children are persuaded to flee the country. Then a family of four manage to get three other refugees out to safety. Somehow the fourteen remaining people have to find enough to eat and drink. Rwandans do not store canned or frozen meals, buying fresh food from the market each day, so there is little in the house to eat. God gives Jean and the family another verse from Proverbs, this time 10:3: 'The Lord will not allow the righteous to hunger.'

Ten metres from the house there is a roadblock and killing post. Day after day the terrible shrieking of people being slaughtered with machetes, clubs and guns reverberates round the house. The family and the others hide in wardrobes and under beds and up the chimney. After four days without food Jean and his youngest daughter, four-year-old Jessie, are in a tiny cupboard and feel chocolate dripping onto them! Wolfgang and Marianne's daughter had been sent this luxury by her grandmother, and it has been stored for a special occasion. Emergency nourishment for the refugees is indeed a special occasion.

Later on God supplies their needs as an avocado tree is blown up in the garden and avocados land on the doorstep to be gathered at night during an 'all-clear'. Mushrooms begin to sprout up from the cement compound, like manna from heaven, freshly replaced each day. The water cistern empties but refills miraculously without any rain, then it empties again after the wet season, and rain falls even through the dry season to replenish their lifeline. God helps them physically too: Jean's sciatic right leg and Viviane's sneezing asthma, both usually exacerbated by cramped conditions, do not trouble them.

Alphonse, the Christian watchman for the house, continues to risk his life insisting to the killers outside the gate that there is no one in the house. This means he has to let them in to use it, and they sit in the lounge boasting of their killings while the family hides in wardrobes. They listen breathlessly as the killers in the next room reel off the names of Jean's friends and relatives whom they have slaughtered.

Five days after taking refuge in the house one of them, a priest, manages to phone an army chaplain for help. But when he is rescued the killers become aware there is a group in the house, and order them all out. They stumble into the glaring sunlight after a week in the dark and are faced with a group of Presidential Guards accompanied by *interahamwe* armed with bows and arrows, spears, guns and grenades. But God quiets Jean's heart and gives him a firm assurance that they are safe.

In a meeting bordering on the surreal, the leader of the killers turns out to be a patient Jean has helped in his medical career. Most loyalties and friendships between hunted and hunter disappeared as soon as the genocide began. Employees betrayed employers, neighbours killed neighbours, friends abandoned friends to be killed. But God's protection remains on Jean and his family (he told the *interahamwe* the whole group was his family), their identity cards are collected and they are told their fate will be decided later. That evening the killers return and one of the group, Claude, who is not of the family, is ordered to lie on the ground. Alphonse the watchman is told he must lie down too, as he is due to be executed for hiding them. Claude is killed but Alphonse is allowed to get up. His Hutu credentials have saved him.

Jean and his family continue to pray that God will confuse the killers and make them forget they are there. Despite the noise of dying all around them, they remain hidden in the house. They endure the screams of a young boy pleading to be finished off as he bleeds to death over three days from machete wounds. They hear the shouts of the killers and their victims as three young men are thrown down a nearby latrine and stoned to death. But a deep-rooted assurance of God's protection continues to fill Jean's heart. Viviane also trusts God, but finds herself amazed at her husband's unshakeable faith. Sometimes Jean sleeps through the chaos outside the house, and in a rare moment of humour Viviane shakes her head and declares: 'You will still be sleeping when you're shot and go sleeping to your death!'

Alphonse brings them snippets of news, and for a while the telephones are working. One of the girls in the group learns her fiancé is dead. Another hears that her parents have been beheaded. Jean and his family hear of the death of relatives. But each day Jean encourages his family to turn to the word of God for help. Three weeks after the start of the genocide he is strongly affected by Psalm 118:17: 'I will not die, but live, and tell of the works of the Lord.' This verse will sustain him for many more weeks, and will later inspire his vow to minister to the survivors.

Three times a day they gather to pray in quiet voices, and then again in the evening to lament before God. One day a mortar shell crashes through the roof and lands in the house. Jean, not being an expert on military matters, is unsure what the smoking contraption is that has landed in his house, and unscrews the shell to try and work out what it is! Incredibly, it fails to explode. The days turn to weeks, the weeks to months, but at last the RPF overrun the city and Jean and his family are freed.

It is a bittersweet freedom after three months of hiding. They are already shattered by their ordeal, but now the full extent of the catastrophe that has hit Jean's family becomes clear. His mother was attacked with a machete and left bleeding for several days in a ditch before she died. His ninety-eight-year-old grandmother was burnt to death and one of his brothers, his wife and five children were thrown into a latrine and buried alive. His father was killed with a sword, and 99 relatives on his father's side were murdered.

Two other brothers and a sister who were living in the south-west are among the forty to fifty thousand who are assured of protection if they run to Murambi school for safety. They crowd into the large grassy compound with its low, brick-built rows of classrooms, surrounded by rolling hills with their patchwork quilt of fields and banana plantations. It is a ruse: they are surrounded until, weakened by hunger and dehydration, they are slaughtered on 21 April, only four escaping alive. In that area of Gikongoro there are other mass graves and memorials, forty-five thousand at one, twenty-five thousand at another, and two others making a hundred and fifty thousand killed in an area of about thirty by ten miles.

Two of Jean's sisters who were married to Hutus have survived, but the other seven siblings are dead. His own survival with his wife and four children is a miracle, and they know it. Not only were they discovered and taken out to be killed, they were also clearly near the top of the death list, since the Presidential Guard were at his door by 6.00 a.m. on the first day of the genocide.

It is not easy to be a minister of comfort after such events. Despite the miraculous intervention of God on many occasions, Jean and his family were left deeply traumatised. In situations of massive shock like this, all natural emotions can leave. The girl who heard her fiancé was dead made no response. The other girl who heard her parents were beheaded just stared blankly into space. When Jean heard of the killing of his parents his only reaction was a dry throat, and for about a year his feelings were completely numbed.

One day in 1995, at a meeting attended by four hundred widows, the dam burst. As Jean listened to their stories and watched their mutilated, blinded bodies weeping with pain, his own heart began to feel again and the tears flowed freely. As the gates of his heart opened up the healing of God began to flow, and with the healing came forgiveness.

With Jean's restoration underway, the time was right to fulfil the vows he had made to God. Together with a local businessman, and with help in the early years from World Relief, he began to organise support for the widows and orphans.

God had taught them many things through the three months of terror: 'We experienced the mercy of God and his faithfulness in a tremendous way; it is true that when you really have faith in him you can never be disappointed. It is also true that in times of crisis true Christians are at their best. Our Lord is a living God, and he hears prayers and answers them.'

Because of the failure of the church to stand against the genocide, the task of ministering to the survivors was made doubly difficult: few trusted anyone connected to the church. Jean made it a principle that they would minister healing first, and help people back to church later. They have now trained hundreds of survivors to comfort and counsel others. Their watchword is: 'We will be able to comfort those who are in any affliction with the comfort with which we ourselves are comforted by God' (2 Cor.1:4).

As a family they are dedicated to helping the survivors. Viviane works in an SOS orphanage and in her
spare time helps with the work at Solace. The children
Ezra, Florence, Mucyo and Jessie live with tremendous
grace and peace, and are a blessing to many. As well as
studying at school and university and working, they
lead orphans' groups and choirs, help in the work of
Solace, and show the beauty of the Lord grown from the
dirty soil of genocide and hatred.

One day I arrived back at Jean's with the four-wheel-
drive. It is a faithful car, tackling the rutted dirt-track
roller-coaster roads of Rwanda's rural hills and valleys,
the clock moving steadily round to its second hundred
thousand kilometres. I had been with a friend at
Akagera Game Park, and we had badly scraped the side
of the car with tough, sharp three-inch acacia thorns. As
we apologised for the damage, Jean waved his hands in
dismissal: 'When you have seen what we have seen and
been through what we have been through, what are
some scratches on a bit of metal?'

There are more important issues on Jean's agenda:
more broken hearts to lead to the healing of the cross,
more empty stomachs to fill, more women with AIDS to
help, more children to educate, more prayer and thanks
and praise to offer God. It is a lifestyle he has promised
to live in obedience to God, and God has given him a
command: 'Be faithful even to the point of death' (Rev.
2:10). Or as Jean says, because it sounds better in
Kinyarwandan: *Ujye ukiranuka, uzageze ku gupfa.*

22

Delivered, Called and Anointed

Those who minister to the widows and orphans have a strong sense of calling because they believe God let them live for a reason. Many are convinced they were seconds away from the strike of the machete or the squeeze of the trigger, and that God specially and miraculously delivered them. It is hard for them to share the burdens of those they minister to. These helpers work through grief and trauma day after day with enough of God's support to counsel effectively. The Bible tells us we are called to mourn with those who mourn, to enter into their sufferings and share their burdens, and the knowledge of that call enables the supporters to assist the healing of the wounded.

Uwimana Sakina Denise works full time counselling and praying with widows and orphans. She knows that God causes all things to work together for good to those who love him and are called according to his purpose, because God began to reveal his purpose to her even while the genocide was going on around her. She is in no doubt that God protected her life for the purpose of ministering to survivors. Denise was born in 1964 in Burundi, where her parents had fled in 1959 to escape the first waves of killing. She grew up in Congo with her Christian family, learning to love God from her father who taught the Sunday School, before returning to Cyangugu in south-west Rwanda in 1987 to get married.

In 1990, when the RPF had given up hope of a peaceful return to their homeland and launched the war, many Tutsis were arrested on the pretext that they were in collusion with the RPF. When the policeman and mayor arrived at Denise's home, she and her husband Charles were kneeling in prayer, crying out to God for the nation. Her husband was imprisoned without trial for six months, and their salaries were stopped. The boss of the cement factory where Charlie worked was a Hutu extremist, and when he was released his boss would not allow him to return to work. He got a job in the capital Kigali and would come at night to visit Denise, dodging the extremists who had now made him a target. Anyone found visiting Denise was put in prison.

During those days, while she questioned why God was allowing such troubles to happen, he gave her a prophetic message through a man of God, a promise she would need to hold on to when the dark days came: 'You are overwhelmed with problems and persecution, but what man cannot do I will do.' The day before the President's plane was shot down, Charlie had left again early in the morning from Cyangugu. It was the last time she saw him. She describes her subsequent deliverance from death with a sense of awe that God preserved her.

A week after the start of the genocide Denise is hiding in the house with nine others and a neighbour is bringing some food for them. 'On 16 April it was our day to be killed,' she states simply. The neighbour arrives with a look of terror and blurts out: 'Do you know what has happened? On the way back from market I saw your aunt, her two boys and your father-in-law killed and lying in the road, and now they are coming to kill you here.' Denise prepares for death by calling her neighbour Goretti to seek forgiveness for not being a better neighbour! 'Please pardon me,' she asked, 'so that we can go to heaven friends.'

Before her neighbour has time to answer there is shooting outside and the *interahamwe* have arrived. Denise is in the house with a brother-in-law, one male cousin, two female cousins, two of her own children, a small girl she has adopted, a boy who has run for his life and found shelter in the house, and a houseboy. The militia start next door with her pregnant neighbour, killing her husband, hacking her son to death, attacking the baby on her back (which somehow survived) and cutting the woman's own head off. Denise calls everyone together and encourages them to seek forgiveness: 'Now we are going to be killed, let us confess our sins before we die.'

There are ten people in Denise's house when the *interahamwe* arrive, but five escape outside and survive. Two of them are her sons and – completely out of character – an *interahamwe* who knows them tells his accomplices to spare them. 'God is even able to put compassion in the heart of a heartless killer,' Denise observes later.

But the other *interahamwe* are smashing down the door and everyone tries to hide. Denise is in the bathroom with her one-year-old son on her back. The *interahamwe* go first to the bedroom, from where Denise hears the helpless screams of her relatives. Then they come to the bathroom and break the door down. Denise is standing there facing a crowd of killers, machetes covered in the blood of her relatives. What she expects to be her last thoughts shoot through her mind: 'God, I'm disappointed in you, why did you not reveal to me that I would die?'

'But God began to protect me, and somehow they did not kill me.' One man raises his machete to kill her, but another stops him and they loot the house then go and kill some others, promising to come back and finish things off at Denise's house later.

Denise has been spared this time, but she is still in danger: other *interahamwe* may return at any time. She crawls under the bed to hide but the floor is drenched with blood, and the groans of those who are not yet dead haunt her through the night until they breathe their last. Denise is pregnant and now is not an opportune time to give birth, but her waters suddenly break and her contractions start. A cousin goes to a neighbour who is a nurse, but her house is guarded to stop her helping the wounded.

Denise and the cousin find a hospital auxiliary who lives nearby, and Denise gives birth in this neighbour's house. About 4.00 a.m. there is more noise as the *interahamwe* return. The auxiliary gives the cousin a stool so that she can hide in the attic, but Denise feels the Holy Spirit prompt her to find refuge in a store-room. The neighbour flees, fearing she may be killed for hiding a Tutsi. *Interahamwe* are everywhere, and Hutu neighbours are ready to betray Denise. The baby has cried briefly at birth, but Denise is amazed that it makes no sound as the killers enter the house to look for survivors. Two grenades thrown into the house fail to explode as the hand of God covers Denise again.

Suddenly God delivers Denise from certain death by the most unlikely means. A soldier of the government, who worked hand in hand with the *interahamwe*, takes her to a dispensary. Denise knows it is a miracle of deliverance, and as she leaves the hospital auxiliary's house she sees her cousin pulled down from the attic and killed. But the *interahamwe* are not happy that

Denise is still alive and they arrive at the dispensary to kill her. One of them draws his arm back to strike her with a sword, but suddenly stops. He sees Denise's two children and takes the sword to kill them, drawing his arm back again to strike, but twice more he is miraculously stopped. He asks what sex the baby is, and a woman in the dispensary winks at Denise to tell him it's a girl, but she cannot tell a lie and says: 'It's a boy.' Again he lifts his arm to strike with his sword, and again it comes down without killing or wounding. Both children have been spared.

'I suffered much but God protected me,' she says. 'They said they would have me for a wife and they came to rape me but God protected me, my body and my children. Some people said I should try and flee but God told me to trust him and stay, and gave me a promise: "If you will indeed stay in this land, then I will build you up and not tear you down . . . do not be afraid . . . for I am with you to save you and deliver you"' (Jer. 42:10-11). Her faith and obedience were vindicated and she and all three of her children survived.

Five years later, in 1999, Denise was still weeping constantly and fighting with God. One day Jean Gakwandi came to her office in Kigali to buy cement. When he saw the Bible on her desk he began to talk to her, and invited her to come and meet others who had been healed. She was still very traumatised and some friends in America wanted her to emigrate there, but as soon as she started to find healing among the widows at Solace she knew God had called her to stay.

The word of God began to bring release to her soul, and instead of bitter tears she began to shed tears of healing. The burden began to lift from her shoulders; she began to remember the promises of God, and faith stirred again in her heart. 'I know God has a plan for me and that is why he delivered me,' she says. She began to gather widows together to pray. The calling was growing, and as her own healing progressed she started to reach out to others. By God's gift many have found healing and salvation through her ministry.

Now Denise is responsible for outreach and evangelism at Solace, and continues to support those who arrive with tearful distress. She is forty-one but is thriving on the ministry God has given her, and looks thirty. Softly-spoken and slightly-built, she is spiritually strong and determined to take back what the enemy has stolen from the widows and orphans who come to her for help.

She has no doubt where the power for her work originates: 'Our ministry is from God and we cannot comfort widows and orphans without the word of God.' It is a recognition that the true Protector of the widow and Father of the fatherless is God, and that his word confirms and proclaims this (Ps. 10:14, 68:5-6, 146:9; Is. 54:5). When such words are received with faith, then healing and hope can enter the widows' and orphans' hearts. 'We have seen how the counselling through the word of God has changed them and helped them to counsel others,' says Denise.

There is a beautiful simplicity in the way transformed people receive the word of God. The wisdom of Proverbs 6:23 illustrates how this works: 'For the commandment is a lamp and the teaching is light; and reproofs for discipline are the way of life.' To receive complete healing a combination of revelation, understanding and repentance are needed to enable someone to respond to the power of the cross. Although Jesus makes it clear that there is no direct link between sin and sickness (Lk. 13:1-5), he suggests that some physical problems may result from unconfessed sin (Mk. 2:1-12, Jn. 5:14).

In his book *Power Healing*[44] John Wimber describes some of the cases where sin and illness are linked, and he highlights unforgiveness and bitterness following trauma. Many afflictions experienced by survivors are clearly injuries or diseases with no spiritual cause, but some survivors associate their pain with unforgiveness, anger or bitterness. When God's word brings light to a survivor, not only can they see the compassion of God, but they are also able to break free from destructive responses to their suffering. The devil hits people with a double punch, the pain itself and the response in our hearts, and the cross frees us from both. When survivors obey the word of God, the results can grow quickly and strongly. This is the beauty of God's word: fruit produced in one person's life can be sown into another. Many who came to Solace broken and lifeless are now ministering to others, sharing healing and hope with them.

There is a beautiful selflessness among those who have been healed. As well as counselling, the widows devote themselves to prayer: 'We are organising prayer cells in the communities, and those who have been helped are called to become intercessors,' Denise explains. 'We pray for the widows and orphans, but we also pray for those who are committed to helping them.' God has put a wonderful gratitude and appreciation in their hearts. Even the younger children of sponsored families fast and pray one day a week in the school holidays, especially for those who sponsor them, and such a gracious attitude makes it a privilege to help them.

23

Hidden Gems

For the survivors of 1994, the battle to find a life of hope continues. New people continue to arrive at Solace week by week in search of healing. Some of those recently arrived are survivors from Bisesero, which is one of the bravest and most tragic stories of the genocide.

Situated just inland from Lake Kivu, a huge lake more than a hundred kilometres long on the western border of Rwanda, Bisesero is in the province of Kibuye. The area is locked in by other provinces to the north, east and south, and with Lake Kivu on the west, once the roadblocks and patrols of the genocide were set up there was no escape route from the massacres. The province, which had the largest Tutsi population of any Rwandan province, probably suffered the highest death rate for Tutsis – about 85 per cent.

The massacres began with many thousands of people killed in the Catholic parish church in the town of Kibuye, and nine thousand more herded into the town's football stadium and also slaughtered.[45] Others, terrified, began to flee to the hills of Bisesero to hide among the rocks and trees.

Daphrose Kandanga,* one of about forty women who survived from the Bisesero hills, remembers the genocide starting during the night of 6 April, almost as soon as the President's plane was shot down. She tells how the mayor's assistant led an attack on an old man and his family and killed them all with grenades. Early the next day the mayor called a meeting to issue instructions for the extermination of the Tutsis. As an example to those at the meeting he took a machete and killed an old Tutsi man. His wife did the same with an old woman. Daphrose remembers the Tutsis being called to a church 'for safety', only to be slaughtered: men, women, children and babies. She herself counts it a miracle she survived with her four children among the dead bodies until darkness came, and they fled.

All around people and cattle were being slaughtered. The women teachers of the local school were tricked into believing they were being led to safety before they were surrounded and raped by gangs of *interahamwe*. Equally shamefully, a local pastor led a group of killers into one of the hospitals where they methodically wiped out the Tutsis.

Within a couple of days, thousands of refugees had gathered on the hills of Bisesero to organise some kind of protection. For two weeks many Hutus and Twa fought alongside local Tutsis against the *interahamwe*, but then they were persuaded to change sides.

The refugees had only sticks, stones, a few spears and some clubs and machetes, whereas their attackers arrived with guns and grenades as well as the ubiquitous machetes and clubs. The only tactic the defenders could employ was to throw stones, or rush among their attackers to reduce their ability to fire guns and throw grenades because of the risk to their own side. The defenders elected leaders to direct the fighting, and even the women and children helped by piling up stones for the men to throw. By now there were forty to fifty thousand Tutsis camped out on the hills. It was the rainy season, and many of them suffered from constant exposure to the cold, wet nights on the hills.

In the early weeks of the resistance it was mainly the men in the front line who died, and the ones who fled were pursued to their hiding-places. Women and children were even less able to run away. Many mothers refused to leave their children, and chose to die with them rather than escape.

Often the fighting lasted most of the day, and as food ran out and their cattle were driven off and slaughtered the defenders grew weaker. By the end of a day's fighting their hands would be raw from throwing stones, their arms aching from the pain. Others would try to hide the corpses of those who had been killed so that those still fighting were not disheartened. As the weeks passed by and each day brought fewer survivors and more corpses, they had neither time nor energy to bury the dead and were forced to abandon their loved ones to the scavenging dogs.

Those who supervised the killing were often community leaders – mayors, councillors, businessmen, pastors and judges. As they met resistance they began to offer financial rewards for people to kill the *Abasesero*, as the Tutsis of Bisesero were known. *Interahamwe* and soldiers arrived together by the bus-load and launched successive attacks, day after day. They also set up a large gun on a nearby hill to fire down on the defenders. The injured had nothing for tending their wounds except rainwater, and many simply lay on the hillside until they were finished off by the attackers another day. The killers had even stolen the crops from fields on the hillside, to deprive them of food. There was nowhere to escape to, and those who tried were inevitably caught at roadblocks and killed. Some took shelter in a local

Adventist church but were attacked by the retired pastor, a leader among the *interahamwe*, who then destroyed the church.

For one week at the beginning of May, four weeks after the killing began, the attacks stopped and people went back to farming their fields. The reprieve was simply a lull while the attackers gathered from Ruhengeri, Byumba, Gisenyi, Cyangugu and Gikongoro to overcome the resistance. On 13 May the *genocidaires* returned with massive forces, determined to wipe out every Tutsi in the area. *Interahamwe*, soldiers and Presidential Guards arrived in buses, lorries and cars, and other militiamen marched along the roads singing songs of the genocide with whistles and drums in the bright red, yellow and green or yellow, blue and black colours of the *interahamwe*, with leaves in their hair, the leaders wearing white shirts.

Alphonse Munyandinda remembers the attack that day:

> Many killers from those regions came to exterminate us. We continued to resist but not as before, and now many people died. Women and children helped the men by handing them stones and sometimes they helped in the fighting, throwing stones at the killers. With their equipment and the support of the army, sometimes we could not resist. It was not easy to fight people with bombs, grenades and guns, and we were overwhelmed. They came among us to finish people who were not completely dead by using machetes and clubs reinforced with nails.

The attack lasted from eight in the morning until four in the afternoon, and the resistance of the refugees crumbled as thousands were killed and the rest tried to break through the lines of attackers to hide in the trees on other hills.

The survivors had to come out at night or in the very early morning to look for family and relatives who had been injured or killed. The women lay naked, stripped of their clothes which were taken for the wives of the killers. In large areas the grass could not be seen for bodies, and many of those who had been killed were badly mutilated or decapitated. The water was red with blood and undrinkable, and the refugees had now been fighting and living rough in the hills for many weeks with only a short respite.

Day after day the attacks continued. Daphrose and her children managed to escape for several weeks but the attackers were relentless in their pursuit of survivors, hunting them down in the bushes with dogs. Her children were eventually found: 'We stayed three weeks in the bush and on 20 June 1994 they discovered my two eldest children, Ntabana and Igihozo. Before killing them, they asked them many questions and tortured them. After that, I took my two youngest children and went to hide in a tea plantation for one week. When we tried to leave there, we met a group of killers and the leader ordered them to kill us. They started with me and beat me with a club until I fell unconscious. When I woke up at 3.00 p.m. I found my two children dead among the other bodies around me.'

By late June, twelve weeks after the first resistance, only two thousand were still alive, emaciated and helpless. On 26 June French soldiers were moving through the area as part of Operation Turquoise. Instead of protecting the survivors, they watched them being killed and then left the *interahamwe* to finish the slaughter for the next three days before returning. By then half of those two thousand had been killed.

Estimates of the final numbers killed vary between thirteen thousand[46] and repeated eye-witness accounts

of forty to fifty thousand victims. 'They killed about
forty-five thousand people,' says Daphrose. The survivors have found it hard to return to the area. Many
hills and forests were littered with remains for years
after the massacres. The hills which used to be covered
with children and cattle are bare, their friends, relatives
and family killed, their homes destroyed and their livelihoods gone. Alphonse, who has recently come to Solace,
summarises their feelings: 'I survived alone in terrible
hardships and have lived alone without parents or
brothers. I continued to live in those conditions without
anyone to talk to. I can say many things but let me stop
here. It is my first time to talk about what happened to
me, and I feel relieved.'

Alphonse and Daphrose have just arrived at Solace
Ministries, and the unwrapping of their hearts from the
layers of shocked sensibilities and frozen memories will
need the deft compassion of the tireless comforters, to
lead them carefully to the healing of the cross. The debt
of pain will take generations to heal in Rwanda, but each
day brings new hope to God's people.

For God's servants at Solace there is a fresh challenge:
to minister to Alphonse and Daphrose. For healing and
reconciliation groups throughout Rwanda, like the one
at Karama, there are more hearts to renew and more sin
to lay at the cross. For pastors like Paul Ndahigwa the
work of discipling and shaping the church continues.
For Alphonse and Daphrose there is the beginning of
hope, a glimpse of light emerging from the chaotic trauma of tangled recollection. For the rest of us, there is the
call to be channels of God's compassion for the widow
and the orphan.

It is April 2006, and Mama Lambert sits at the Gisozi
memorial on the day of mourning which commemorates
the genocide each year. Poignant pictures of children

who died in the genocide are shown on a large screen in honour of the many thousands whose laughs and smiles will never again touch their parents' hearts. It is not often Mama Lambert cries now, but as the image of one of her own five murdered children fills the screen her tears flow freely again. Those who died are not forgotten, the memory of their helpless last moments stirring the embers of love in a mother's heart. But tomorrow Mama Lambert will be back comforting and counselling others, her warm smile returning to her face. And tomorrow, because of God's gracious love and the help of his people, Constance and her family will have food on their table, Philomena and her family will have a roof over their heads, Alexis will build homes for widows with a cleansed heart, and Ruth will dance before the Lord.

Albert Tumubare was nine when his mother and brother were killed among thousands of others at Ntarama Church. He does not know where his sister was killed, but he saw his father bludgeoned to death with machetes in front of his eyes. The aunt he stayed with was crippled in the fighting and died later. 'After the genocide I could not pray,' he says. 'All my neighbours were involved in the genocide and I hated them, always thinking of revenge and planning to kill them. But since I met Solace Ministries and participated in their prayer meetings, I feel a thirst to pray. I'm saved, I love Jesus and I'm now a youth leader. People have told me I have a gift to be a pastor, but sometimes I feel discouraged and worried. We still have trauma and we need more prayer.' Such exceptional people continue to need love and support.

'The Lord . . . supports the fatherless and the widow,' says Psalm 146. Pure religion is when we do the same, says God's word. When Gahongayire

Donatilla knew her story would be included in this book, she finished her contribution with an eloquent appeal for support:

'I have finished my testimony and I call you readers to pray and support the suffering survivors of the genocide in Rwanda. Many thanks for those who already support us in many ways. May God bless your families, business and your countries.'

May God help us, wherever we find the suffering, the widows and the orphans, to be his hands and his heart, and minister to them with his love and peace.

Endnotes

[1] There are many statistics quoted concerning the number of people killed in genocides during the twentieth century. Those sometimes include the 30-50 million killed during the Chinese cultural revolution, many dying from famine, and the twenty million that died under Stalin in the USSR, Cambodia (about two million), Armenia (1.5 million) and the Nazi Holocaust (fourteen million) are the best known of the other large genocides but websites such as *Death Tolls for the Major Wars and Atrocities of the 20ᵗʰ Century* – users.erols.com, *Genocide in the 20ᵗʰ Century* – historyplace.com and others provide information on many other atrocities.

[2] Asterisked names have been changed to preserve anonymity, non-asterisked names have not been changed. Rwandans generally use a Christian name and a Rwandan name, but surnames are rarely used.

[3] Romeo Dallaire speaking at the Edinburgh Book Festival 2005.

[4] A 2004 census accounted for 937,000 killed, but estimates using census data, remains of those killed and other investigation results in Rwandan government publications now saying 'more than one million.'

[5] Romeo Dallaire, *Shake Hands With the Devil* (London: Arrow Books, 2003), p. 548.

6 Meg Guillebaud, *After the Locusts* (Oxford: Monarch Books, 2005).

7 Lesley Bilinda, *Colour of Darkness* (1996) and *With What Remains* (2006) (both London: Hodder & Stoughton).

8 Frank Smyth, *The Horror,* 20 June 1994.
   www.franksmyth.com.

9 Chrétien et al., *Rwanda, Les medias du Genocide* (Paris: Karthala, 1995).

10 The ten commandments were well known throughout the Hutu power movement and can be seen at the Gisozi Memorial, Kigali. They were published in December 1990 in the *Kangura* newspaper (6), which was financed by the Information Bureau of President Habyarimana to promote the ethnic cleansing message.

11 *The New Times*, Kigali, 28-29 December 2005; also: *Lettre ouverte à M. Jacques Chirac, Président de la Republique Francaise* from FIDH (Federation Internationale des Ligues des Droits de l'Homme), 7 April 2004. www.fidh.org; also: Registry of the European Court of Human Rights, 285, 8 June 2004, www.echr.coe.int Chamber judgements.

12 Justus Iyamuremye, *The New Times*, 4 January 2006.

13 Hassan Ngeze, *Gisenyi: Kangura* newspaper (52), January 1994.

14 Gregory Stanton, *The Eight Stages of Genocide*, first written in 1996 at the US Department of State, now explained in *The Eight Stages of Genocide: How Governments Can Tell When Genocide Is Coming and What They Can Do To Stop It* (Washington DC: Genocide Watch, 2001).

15 United Nations, *Rwanda – UNAMIR Background*,
    www.un.org, Department of Peacekeeping Operations.

16 Security Council Resolution 935(1994).

17 Action memorandum from Assistant Secretary of State for African Affairs George E. Moose, Assistant Secretary of State for Democracy, Human Rights and Labor John Shattuck, Assistant Secretary of State for International

Organisation Affairs, Douglas J. Bennett, and Department
of State Legal Advisor Conrad K. Harper, through Under
Secretary of State for Global Affairs Peter Tarnoff and
Under Secretary of State Tim Wirth, to Secretary of State
Warren Christopher: *Has Genocide Occurred in Rwanda?* 21
May 1994. Secret. See www.africaaction.org. Also:
Carlsson, Sung-Joo and Kupolati, *Report of the Independent
Inquiry into the Actions of the United Nations during the
1994 genocide in Rwanda* (New York: UN, 1999).
www.un.org/news.

[18] Philip Verwimp, 'Testing the double genocide thesis for
central and southern Rwanda', *Journal of Conflict Resolution*
Vol. 47 No. 4, Aug. 2003).

[19] Edwin Musoni '28,000 Leaders Implicated in Genocide',
New Times, 21 Dec. 2005.

[20] Charles Mironko, *Iberto: Means and Motive in the Rwandan
Genocide*, Yale University, 2004.

[21] Leaflet given personally by Archbishiop Kolini in 1999.

[22] Copy of confession given personally by participant – the
document can be viewed on www.ukuli.org.

[23] Administered by worshiptogether.com songs, excluding
UK and Europe, administered by kingswaysongs.com
tym@kingsway.co.uk.

[24] Duncan Morrow, 'Forgiveness and Reconciliation' in B.
Hamber, D. Kule and R. Wilson, *Future Policies for the Past*
(Belfast: *Democratic Dialogue*, Feb. 2001), p. 15-29.

[25] Charlene Smith, *Proud of Me* (Johannesburg: Penguin
Books, South Africa 2001).

[26] *Ibid.*

[27] Office National de la Population 1998: p. 18.

[28] Study carried out by AVEGA Widows' Association in 1999.

[29] The practice of buying a bullet was widespread during the
genocide. The cost varied – for example Muzungu Gon-
zague was taken to a pit latrine at Ruyumba and was about
to be killed with machetes when he pleaded for a bullet. 'A

bullet is expensive,' he was told, but he bought a swift death for 35,000 Rwandan francs (about £45). Most could not afford that.

30 Gayle Cullinan in *Australian Society for Traumatic Stress Studies, Newsletter* December 2003, p. 19.
31 Frank Retief, *Tragedy to Triumph* (Cape Town: Struik Christian Books, 1994).
32 Meg Guillebaud, *Rwanda: The Land God Forgot?* (London: Monarch Books, 2002).
33 Fergal Keane, *Massacre at Nyarubuye Church,* news.bbc.co.uk, Sunday 4 April 2004.
34 Susan Hunter and John Williamson, *Children on the Brink, Updated Estimates,* US Agency for International Development 2000, The Synergy Project.
35 www.unicef.org/infobycountry/rwanda.
36 David Cormack, *Peacing Together* (London: Monarch Publications, 1989).
37 Instructions of the Executive Secretary of the National Service of Gacaca Courts, Number 6, 2005.
38 Organic Law No. 40/2000. Published 26 January 2001. Government of Rwanda.
39 Paul Kagame, *Frontline: Ghosts of Rwanda,* www.pbs.org 1 April 2004.
40 Robert Carkhuff, *Helping and Human Relations* (Amherst, MA: Human Resource Development Press, 1984).
41 Augustine of Hippo, *Tractate 3 on the Gospel of John.* See www.newadvent.org.
42 E.J.M. Shirima, 'Benefits from dual purpose for crop and livestock production under small-scale peasant systems in Kondoa eroded areas, Tanzania', *Livestock Research for Rural Development* 17 (12), 2005.
43 Global Aids Programme, Rwanda Country Profile, www.cdc.gov.
44 John Wimber and Kevin Springer, Power Healing (London: Hodder & Stoughton, 1986).

45 Philip Verwimp, 'Death and survival during the 1994 genocide in Rwanda', *Population Studies* Vol. 58, No. 2, 233-245.
46 Philip Verwimp, *Ibid*.

comfort
international
a little can change a life

Royalties from the sale of this book will be forwarded by
Comfort International (previously Comfort Rwanda) to our
partners in Rwanda.

Comfort International was established in 1999 to support
the work of local Christian Rwandans in their recovery
from the genocide. It works with Solace Ministries, an
organisation dedicated to the healing and support of
survivors from the genocide, and with *L'Église Vivante*
(The Living Church) and the Healing and
Reconciliation Programme.

Funds have been used for school fees and materials,
trauma healing camps, the purchase of goats and cattle,
building or buying houses for homeless widows or
orphans, food relief during periods of drought, Bibles,
sewing machines, computers, bicycles, and support for
church training programmes. There is a sponsorship
scheme for orphans and child-headed households.

Information can be obtained from:

Comfort International,
23 Lochty Street
Carnoustie, DD7 6EE
www.comfort.international

enquiry@comfort.international

The same address can be used to contact the author for
speaking engagements.